Filey

A History of The Town and its People.

W.M. Rhodes

Filey A History of The Town and its People.

W.M. Rhodes ©2022.

A copy of this book has been deposited with the British Library.

ISBN-Hardback Edition

978-1-8381769-8-3

ISBN 978-09957752-4-4

ISBN 978-09957752-0-6

ISBN 978-09957752-8-2

ISBN 978-1-8381769-9-0

ISBN 978-1-8381769-2-1

First Edition 19th May 2017

Second Edition July 2018.

Updated New Edition July 2022

Dedication

I dedicate this book to the people who have lost their lives at sea and the brave volunteers who risk their own lives attempting to rescue them.

What though the sea be calm

Trust to the shore; Ships have been drown'd

Where late they danced before.

(Robert Herrick)

Contents

Acknowledgements

This is the new edition of *Filey's A History of the Town and Its People.* I wanted to add a couple more stories and photographs to this version.

I want to express my appreciation to all the people who permitted me to reproduce photographs for this book. Some pictures are old and out of copyright, and they do not reprint well because of their age. Thank you to Edward Waterson for inspiring me to research and write the story of North Cliff Villa and Miss Elinor Clarke.

Thank you to the team—editor Maureen Vincent-Northam, the formatting team, and all at La-di Dah publishing.

To Jasmine-Our Angel. Forever in our hearts.

To my husband, Paul. Children: Kristian, Becky, Zoe, their partners and all our grandchildren.

A special thanks to my parents, Denise & Horace. I miss you both every day.

W. M Rhodes.

Filey 2022.

Filey's Roman Presence

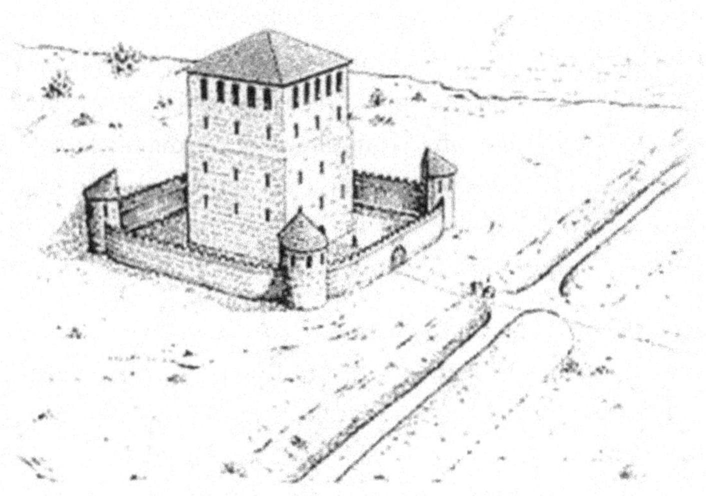

Arguably, one of the most significant events in Britain is the Roman invasion. For over four hundred years (and still evident today), the Romans have influenced our language, culture, architecture and geography. Before the Roman occupation, Britain had a diminished sense of identity. People tended to be insular and stayed close to their local tribes. After the Romans came to town, inhabitants knew that their national mythology was defined, and every person in the land was mindful of their 'Britishness'. In addition, the Welsh knew they were Britain's natural heirs. The Scots and the Irish were equally proud that they were not conquered and occupied by the Romans.

The Romans built towns and connected them by building roads to administer their people. So well-built were these roads that many remain today. Romans constructed the roads on foundations of clay, chalk and gravel. They then laid flat stones on top. These roads sloped in the middle to man-made ditches on either side to allow rainwater to drain. Roads were built as straight as possible to enable Roman soldiers to travel quickly, ensuring no enemies were hiding in unseen winding areas.

In Yorkshire, the main Roman town was Eboracum (York as we know it today). Malton was a Roman garrison named Derventio, a town of great importance and a base for troops who could easily be deployed if required. The Romans built walls around their cities to protect themselves from land invasion, preventing fierce barbarian attacks from tribes such as The Huns from Mongolia and Germanic Tribes from the Danube River. The Romans built early warning lookout stations along the coast to protect their towns from an invasion by sea. These stations could signal each other and alert any sign of danger.

For many years, renowned archaeologists have written articles and journals to prove that Filey Bay was the Portus Felix or Sinus Salutaris of the Romans and that Flamborough Head, the Ocellum Promontorium. However, theorists continue to debate these issues. Further speculation remains that Filey was the territorial home to one of the Celtic Parisi tribes (there were four in the North). The Parisi was a small group of people who farmed Yorkshire's chalk hills and traded by boat, most probably a longboat. As a tribe, the Parisi were not as powerful as their neighbours, the Brigantes but were ahead in culture and taught their unrefined neighbours about style and culinary matters. The Parisi lived in British-style houses with ornaments and pottery.

The Parisi tribe was originally from Gaul and shared their name with the people who lived in France around the area we know today as Paris. Despite being responsible for the French capital's name, it is unclear if they shared any other links with the French. This tribe was distinctive, as unlike many others living in Britain between 300 and 100 B.C., the Parisi buried their dead under small barrows surrounded by small ditches. The burial of some nobles was with their chariots. This method is associated with the 'Arras' culture and has a similar style to the French and Germans. Another burial style involved a dead person put in a grave and a fine sword placed alongside him, with three spears thrust into his chest. These unusual burial rituals ceased around 43-45AD. The Parisi was an ununiformed tribe. Along with their neighbours, the Brigantes, who did not defend themselves against the arrival of the Romans.

Reports show that the Romans once occupied Filey during their invasion of England in October 1857. After weeks of severe rain, a landslip occurred on Carr Naze. Three hundred yards from 'The Summer House.' (Once an attraction of the 'Spaw Well' on Carr Naze in the mid-nineteenth century) and close to the second flight of steps beyond Agony Point, when a painter named Mr Jeffrey Wilson discovered the remains of a Roman Fort. Here, he uncovered large stones in a rough state with tooled surfaces on a foundation of puddled clay. This walled area was rectangular and about 60 feet long by 25 feet wide, with one door opening to the land.

Within these walls were five shaft base stones, one with a carving of a running deer and on a second a calf about to lie down. Also found were the remains of burnt wood, a spearhead, with burnt bones, which lay on the floor, together with a piece of shale or shaly slate inscribed, CAESAR SE... and QVAM SPE. Coins were discovered, which were brass and had significantly become corroded. Press reports suggest these coins bore the mark of Constantine and Constans.

Strategically placed beacons were arranged at the corners of a square measuring about 17 feet with one stone in the centre. Most likely, these stones would have formed the bases for pillars that rested a superstructure. Most probably, there was a raised platform which supported a lighted beacon. Conceivably, the beacon's attendant and his family lived nearby to light the beacon when required and keep it bright and strong to carry a signal north and south to warn the ancient mariner of the dangerous rocks and welcome back the midnight wanderer.

On discovery, the Roman structure had been severely damaged and then set on fire, suggesting that it had been overwhelmed by raiders, presumably from the sea. These five stones are displayed in The Crescent Gardens and show that a Roman township existed in the area.

The following year, Rev. Richard Burke, the then-owner of Carr Naze, allowed local antiquarian Dr William Smithson Cortis to excavate his land. To the south-eastward of the Spa Well, Cortis unearthed various pottery typical of the Roman era, one with a green glaze and a larger wine vase formed from red clay ornamented with painted scrolls. One piece of Samian was unearthed, together with buckles, pins, a part of a sword, a sharpening stone, beads, etc. Unfortunately, what has happened to these artefacts is not known.

In 1893, Mr Robert M Robson wrote in the Journal of the Society of Architects of discovering nine oak posts found on Filey Brigg by Messrs. R & W Cappleman. This discovery suggested that the posts were the remains of a landing stage used by the Romans when Filey was one of their mooring stations. He also implies that there is other evidence pointing to this, such as the Roman Roads, Spittal Rocks, Fess Rocks, Quay Rocks, and the artificially flattened surface of the Binks on the north side of the bay. However, despite these findings, there is no definite confirmation that Roman occupation existed in Filey.

Roman stones (Crescent Gardens)

Domesday and Early Settlement

The earliest documented evidence of Filey comes from The Domesday Book, compiled in 1068 CE on the instructions of William the Conqueror primarily for tax. This review was known as the 'great survey of England' and determined how much land and livestock each of the counties' landowners owned, how much it was worth, and how much tax they should pay. These records show that at the end of the Viking period, Filey was recorded for the first time as a tiny village occupied by less than fifty people. It states that Filey was worth a reasonable income, with access to good quality timber ideal for construction.

The Norman Conquest found Filey belonging to the rebellious Earl Tostig. The Domesday survey described Filey as forfeited to the King and was by him given to one of his faithful followers and relatives, Walter de Gant, who was born in 1080 in Bridlington.

It is impossible to know how old Filey is. Reports suggest that it may have been between 878 and 1080 or earlier. It is known that the Danes settled in the North between 878-1080. Therefore, there is a possibility that this North Germanic tribe, who originally came to England as Vikings, discovered Filey. However, Filey was one large farm. The name Filey suggests it had more of an Anglican influence than a Danish one, as farms founded by Danes usually ended with the suffix 'by' such as Whitby or Selby. So, this could mean that the Danes did not have the influence in Filey as first thought. However, this is not conclusive.

Interestingly, we can detect a strong Scandinavian influence in the dialect of many Filey people, for instance, in terms such as 'garth' meaning garden, '-uh-wand' as an expression of surprise or 'where-be-orbit' meaning who or where do you come from? Maybe the Danish Vikings figure more in the ancestry of Filey than we first thought. We can certainly see the Norse influence in the fishing cobles used by the Filey fishermen, who adopted the Danish skill of boatbuilding by using the 'clinker' method of building which involved the overlapping of planks of wood in constructing sea-worthy boats.

Reports suggest that there once stood an ancient Saxon church dedicated to St Bartholomew during the Middle Ages. This church was most likely behind the present church (St Oswald's). However, by the 16th century, this church was in ruins. There is no further physical evidence to suggest anything happening in Filey until the building of St. Oswald's Church, around 1150 CE. Thus, there is a gap in our knowledge of any recorded activity in Filey for five centuries. Roughly between 500 and 1,000 CE.

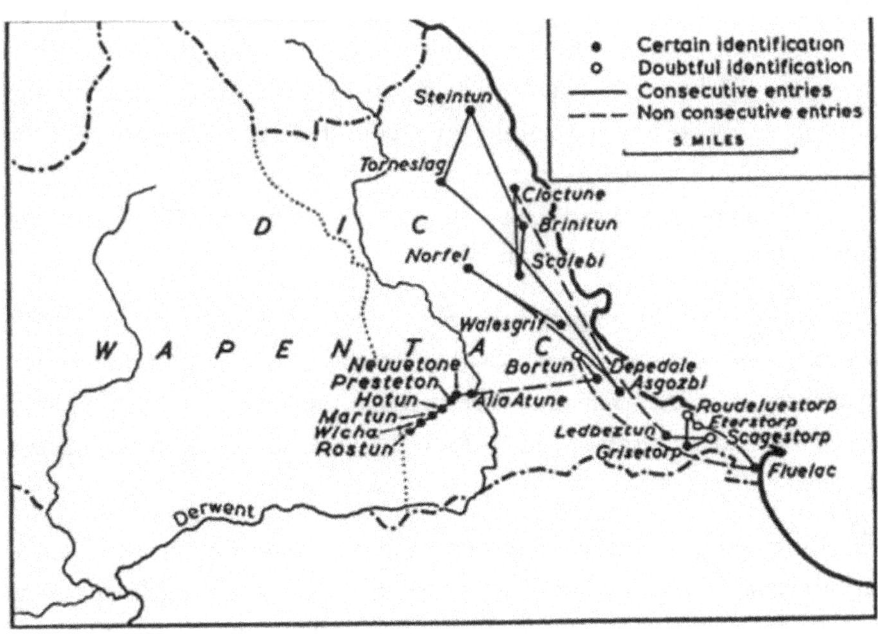

North Filey - The Buck and The Beckwith Families

As discussed we do not know what happened in Filey between 500 and 1000 CE. However we know that St Oswald's church was built around 1150, but there is only a sparse understanding of the beginnings of Filey's community.

There is no mention of a monastery or a church in the Domesday book for Filey. Therefore, we can assume that the leaders built the church to serve an existing Filey community. Nowadays, the church is isolated to the North of Church Ravine, dividing it from the rest of the town and the community. It is not feasible for a church of this magnitude to be built on the 'wrong' side of the tracks, where no population lives. After all, Filey inhabitants would have had to climb steep cliffs to attend church, which doesn't seem workable.

According to the historian John Cole, there are old records (which he does not specify) which speak of the North and south of Filey as two separate entities and that there are many foundations of old buildings near St Oswald's church. [1]However, no documentation exists to confirm this.

Over the years, excavations have attempted to determine if a church or manor house existed on land to the North of Filey. In 1927, surveyors Clay, Robson and Smith carried out an archaeological dig of the area.

---

1 Cole. J. The Antiquities of Filey. 1827.

The results showed a possibility of a manor house in this area possibly belonging to the Buck family. Reports suggested this manor house could have been the same place Church Cliff Farm is now. Also, there was an original smaller church, with the possibility that St Oswald's was built directly on top of the original Filey church. Further excavations took place in Queen Street in the 1970s, revealing medieval remains.

However, there is still a significant gap in Filey's history between the three hundred years from the building of St Oswald's Church to the community of Queen Street (King Street, Town Street), Filey's oldest recorded street.

Land immediately in front of Church Cliff Farm. Could this be the place of Filey's original settlement?

Excavations at Church Cliff Farm.

The Bucks & The Beckwith's

It is stated that a manor house in 'north Filey' could have belonged to the Buck family. Later, records show that Sir John Buck of Hamby-Grange was knighted by King Charles 1st with several others at Whitehall on 23rd July 1603 before his majesty's coronation. John Buck married Elizabeth Green, the daughter and heir of William Green Esq of Filey. The couple lived at Hamby Grange, Leverton, Lincolnshire. John Buck held the office of Sheriff of Lincolnshire from 1619 to 1620 and later became Sheriff of York. The couple had a son named John Buck, who married three times. He received the title of 1st Baronet Buck of Hamby Grange, co. Lincoln [England] on 22 December 1660. He also held the office of Sheriff of Lincolnshire from 1663 to 1664.

The Beckwith's derived their name from Lady Dame Beckwith Bruce, daughter of Sir William Bruce, the third Lord of Annandale, whose Lordship and lands he had inherited from his ancestor. Dame was also the half-sister of Sir Robert, the Bruce of Skelton Castle, the progenitor of the Royal Bruce of Scotland. Her father, William de Bruce, possessed large estates in the North of England. Lady Beckwith Bruce inherited an estate or manor of land called Beckwith in the old Anglo-Saxon Beckworth from 'Beck', a brook and 'Worth'. In 1226, Dame married Sir Hercules de Malebisse and requested that her husband change his name by deed to Beckwith upon her marriage. Sir Hercules was the great-grandson of Sir Hugo de Malebisse c. 1066, who held lands in the time of William the Conqueror.

Adam Beckwith, Lord of Clint (b.1405), married Elizabeth de Malebisse (b. 1406) and thus united the two branches of the De Malebisse families after a separation of over three hundred years. Adam was the son of Thomas Beckwith. The couple's eldest son Sir William married the daughter of Sir John Baskerville, who was succeeded by his son Thomas Beckwith of Clint. Thomas married the daughter and co-heiress of W. M Haslerton. He then became Lord of the Manor of Filey, Muston and Thorp, which his wife had inherited from Havisia, the daughter and co-heiress of Ralph de Neville.

Another branch of the Beckwith family was Mathew Beckwith of Tanfield, a captain in the Parliamentary Army. Mathew married Elizabeth Buck of Filey, the daughter of John Buck. The couple did not live in Filey but in Tanfield, where Mathew died in 1679. It is interesting to see how these families are connected and their influence in the small town of Filey.

Filey: Origins of its Name

The origins of the name 'Filey' are not precisely known. Maybe it originated from the word Fucelac meaning 'the bay where the birds are.' However, historians dispute this theory suggesting the misreading of the spelling. Thus, according to Sir Henry Ellis's edition of the Domesday Book. The name Fiuelac is the correct spelling. It refers to 'five pools', which includes 'The Emperor's Bath' in which Constantine the Great is believed to have bathed over one thousand and seven hundred years ago (an unsubstantiated claim). Interestingly, the suffix 'lac' is an ancient Northumbrian word for wood, which confirms the findings written in this famous book. Also, there was a great forest in 'Scalby' supporting this.

Over the years, there have been further claims to the origin of the name. It was 'Fyvele' then 'Fyveley' in the thirteenth century. Some suggested the name was Fay-ley, meaning the fairies' home, Fif and laeh, or Five-Leys, meaning *five clearings*. One interesting suggestion was that the name derived from 'Fifel', meaning monster or the devil. Fifel-Leah is a place haunted by demons. Indeed, the Brigg could be haunted by demons. Its unrelenting, treacherous rocks have taken many ships and sailors' lives.

When this 'great survey' was written, the jurisdiction for the lands attached to Filey was in the manor of *Walesgrif* (*Falsgrave* as we know it today). Here is an extract from the Domesday Book, translated from Latin.

'There are in Walesgrif and in the hamlet of Nordfield 15 geldable (i.e. taxable) carucates of land, which will be cultivated by 8 ploughs. (Tosti [brother of King Harold] held these as one manor. Now the King's). There are within this manor 5 villans who have two carucates. There is wood, with pasturage three miles in length and two miles in breadth. In the time of King Edward, the value was fifty-six pounds. To this, the manor had the jurisdiction of the following lands. Azgodbi (4 carucates) Ledberston, Grieftorp, Scagetorp, Eterstrop, Rodbestrop, Facelac, Bertune, Depedale, Atune, Neuveton, Prestetune, Hortune, Marlane, Wicham, Rosture, Tornelai, Stentun, Brinnistin, Scaltebi, Cloctune.

There are 84 carucates of geldable land cultivated with 42 ploughs. Upon these lands, there were 17 socmen and 15 villans, 14 borders, with 7 carucates and a half. The rest of the land is waste.'

The Gristhorpe Man

In July 1834, a local landowner William Beswick dug into a barrow on a cliff near Filey. He discovered an ancient British cairn or tumulus. Inside, he exposed a perfectly preserved skeleton, stained black with oak tannins. The skeleton was wrapped in animal skin and surrounded by a drinking cup, a bronze dagger and flints. The skeleton was a six-foot man crushed into a minimal space so that his knees nearly touched his chin.

The man had a remarkable muscular physique. He also had a well-developed cranium which showed that he possessed exceptional mental power. Identification of the skeleton found it was a Bronze Age warrior chieftain who lived over 4000 years ago, now known worldwide as 'The Gristhorpe Man'. At the time of the discovery, Mr Gage, the Antiquarian Society's treasurer, supervised the tumulus's opening. The skeleton's bones were so brittle that they fell to pieces immediately after being exposed to the air and had to be carefully handled.

The skeleton is on view at Rotunda Museum in Scarborough. In 2005, Bradford University re-examined the remains and found:

'The Gristhorpe Man is one of the tallest men known in Britain from the Early Bronze Age and received a prestigious burial. Isotope analysis of a tooth showed he originated from the Scarborough area and ate a lot of meat when he was young. Radiocarbon dating of the tooth dentine has demonstrated that he died around 4000 years ago (CT scanning of the skull).

The Bradford team analysed the artefacts buried with the body, including metallurgical and isotope analyses of the dagger blade, analysis of the bark container and its contents, and a re-assessment of the 'mistletoe berries' and micro-ware on the flint knife. A study of the coffin lid looked at its uniqueness.

'face' carved at one end and dendrochronological and radiocarbon dating of the tree rings provided a date for the oak coffin.

In addition, the team carried out geophysical surveys and a small excavation on the original discovery site. These have located the 19th-century dig and revealed details of the barrow construction and its preservation. We took pollen samples that enabled us to build up a picture of the local environment at Gristhorpe 4000 years ago,' [2]

Towards the end of the nineteenth century, a skeleton of a large deer with magnificent antlers was dug out of the cliffs at Filey. The skeleton was either that of a fallow deer or a red deer. It must have belonged to the glacial period, or if the latter, it would date back to around 500 BC. Unfortunately, no records are available to confirm which one it was.

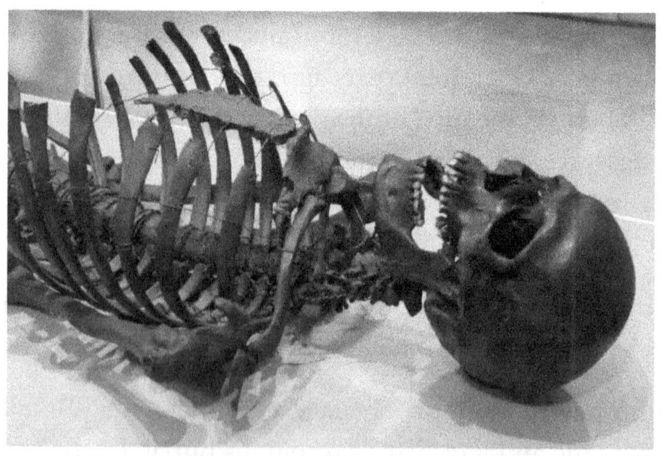

Skeleton of The Gristhorpe Man

---

2 Bradford University, 2005

Filey Enclosure

An Act of Parliament in 1791 permitted the dividing, allotting, and enclosing of the several open and common arable fields, meadows, pastures, commons and waste grounds of the township of Filey. Before this act, Filey used the Middle Ages system commonly adopted throughout England, whereby land was worked by the community and divided into aggregated strips, worked on three fields on a rotation system, which allowed each field to lay fallow every 2, 3 or 4 years. These strips were owned or tenanted by the villagers. The division of the strips varied considerably but would be about a furrow long (220 yards) in length and a few yards wide. (Country Park retains clear indications of strip farming, as does a part of Glen Gardens.)

The primary purpose of Enclosure was to improve the efficiency of agriculture. However, there were other motives, usually small farmers working together, leading to the enclosure of whole parishes.

The establishment of clear titles to land was convenient and a significant factor in the ease of acquiring land. Land values had increased, and beneficiaries of the act sold the land for housing in what would later become known as 'New Filey.' (The Crescent)

Before the Enclosure Act, Filey had three fields:

Great Field: The land that now houses Scarborough Road.

Church Field: To the North of St. Oswald's – what is now Country Park.

Little Field: Both sides of what is now West Avenue.

According to working-class politics of the late 18th and 19th centuries, the Enclosure Act stole people's land. The land they had worked for many years. Thus, leaving people impoverished and destroying the small farmers' agrarian way of life - a life that had sustained families for centuries. Before the act, English agriculture depended on common land that was privately owned but to which others enjoyed the right of legal access.

Following this new Act of Parliament, commissioners appointed by the government distributed Filey land. John Dickenson, who was well known as an honest man (he was a Quaker), completed the survey for Filey and concluded that there were -

695 Acres, I rood, 12 perches (a perch is about 30 square yards.)

Besides the redistribution of the arable land, the main highways, i.e., Muston Road, Scarborough Road, Sand Road (Murray Street), Great Carr Goat Road (Ravine Hill) and Cottagers Road (West Road, as far as the Junior School) were widened, with attention given to the current drainage system.

The division of the land was:

Humphrey Osbaldeston – 376 acres.

Michael Newton – 122 acres.

Christopher Foster – 101 acres.

Thomas Robinson – 15 acres.

Robert Rowe – 16 acres.

Elizabeth Huntress – 8 acres.

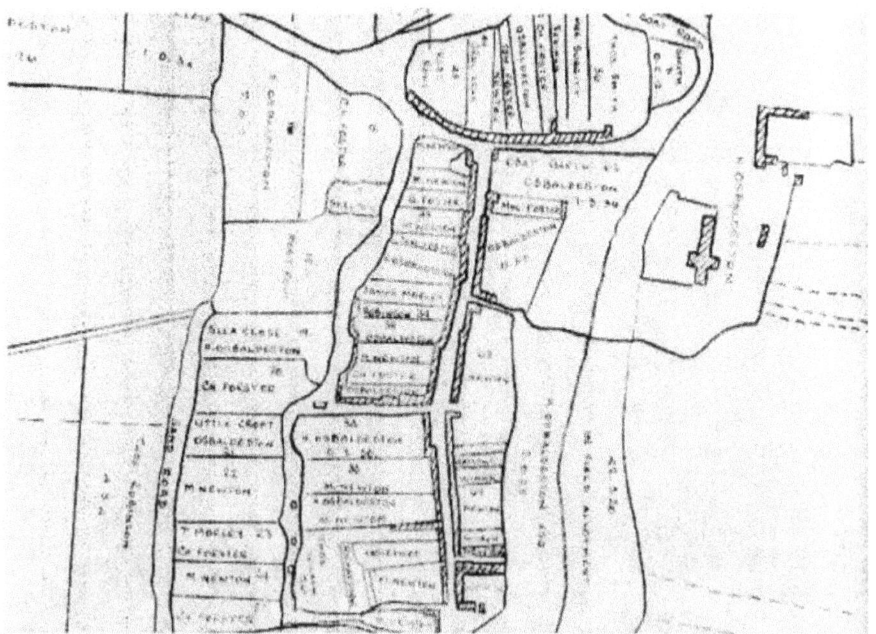

1791 Enclosure Map

Filey Brigg

Credit Stephen Eblet

Filey Brigg, or 'Bridge' as it was sometimes known, is a rocky peninsula extending almost 1.5 km along the north side of Filey Bay and lies 1 km northeast of Filey town. The rocks vary from pure sandstone to limestone, created by tiny sea creatures invisible to the naked eye. Filey Brigg is a haven for geologists and ornithologists with fossiliferous rocks and ledges. The Brigg is ideal for birdwatching, angling, and fossil hunting. People spend many hours enthusiastically exploring this natural environment, looking for birds such as the Herring Gull, Sand Martins or Kittiwakes.

Credit Stephen Eblet

The waves have cut out holes in the cliff face because the strata's angle
is exposed on the peninsula's north side. These holes, or shallow caves,
are called 'doodles.' They each have names such as First Doodle, Second

Doodle, Long Doodle and Far Doodle. Above the water level is a hard rock layer with a softer layer containing 'balls' (hard siliceous masses) above it. Over the years, the waves have washed out these balls, which rolled around, eroding the rock surface beneath them and creating a 'bath'. Many rock pools on the Brigg, including 'The Emperor's Bath' and the treacherous 'Black Hole'. The Black Hole is aptly named as it is far more profound than it looks to the naked eye. It also marks the end of the road for anyone attempting to walk on the seashore to Scarborough.

Emperor's Pool and Fishing on The Brigg

In mid-Victorian times, if you wanted to go on the Brigg as a visitor, you would be besieged by a dozen boys asking, 'carriage sir, take you to the Brigg for a shilling!' And they would be back to collect you in two hours.

Carriages waiting to take visitors to the Brigg

The days of youths meeting trains and taking visitors on the Brigg are long gone. However, the one thing that will never change is that the Brigg can be a dangerous place. People should take extreme caution when walking on the Brigg as many areas are slippery, the cliffs are crumbly, and you must monitor the incoming tides, which creep up on you unexpectedly. It is vital to follow the warnings and stay safe.

Many people have met their death on the Brigg through the years, even at low tide, as the big waves and rough sea sprays have swept them off their feet. Not realising the force of the fast-flowing tides, others are left stranded and trapped and need to be rescued by the Coastguard. Here are a few examples:

In September 1818, twenty-five-year-old William Oddie from Woodlesford, near Leeds, was holidaying in Scarborough with two of his friends. They took a boat from Scarborough to Filey. The weather was fine, and they arrived at Filey 'Bridge' shortly after midday. They went ashore and spent an hour exploring the rocks and scenery. Then went back to their boat to return to Scarborough. Ten minutes later, a gust of wind plunged the boat underwater – they all clung to the wreck except for Mr Oddie, who swam to the shore. However, his heavy overcoat and full-length leather boots encumbered him. Thus, he could not reach his destination. Panicking, he swam back to the boat where his friends were still holding on. His hope and stamina waned when he got within twenty yards of them. With his strength gone, he let out a shriek and disappeared. The other two men were rescued shortly afterwards by a sloop, who took them back to Scarborough.

Unfortunately, Mr Oddie remains another statistic of the relentless sea.

One of the saddest drowning cases on the Brigg happened in October 1871, when Doctor Haworth was shooting birds on the Brigg (how times change) with his two sons and one of their friends. The doctor shot a bird, and his son Joseph climbed onto a rock to reach it when a sudden wave came and washed him into deep water. Although his father was within a few yards of him, he could not reach him. To make matters worse, the family's pet dog, a golden retriever, rushed into the sea to save his master. Unfortunately, the dog placed his paws on Joseph's body, which caused him to sink. The poor boy's body was recovered shortly afterwards by local fishermen.

In a secluded commemorative corner of Filey Parish churchyard (St Oswald's) and graced by weeping willows, marks a small cross, which serves as a memorial to twelve sailors who, in January 1871, were far away from their homeland and their loved ones, lost their lives. They drowned at sea when a coal-laden Italian Barque named *The Unico*, heading between Newcastle and Constantinople, struck violently against the rocks on Filey Brigg. The vessel shattered on impact. Only the captain of a crew of thirteen survived.

This and similar tragedies posed the question of building a Harbour of Refuge at Filey. Hopefully, this would help prevent similar disasters to the ill-fated *Unico*.

Agony Point

In 1873, Mr Paget, the retired MP for Nottinghamshire and his wife Ellen tragically drowned as they stood on a ledge close to 'Emperor's Bath' when a huge wave washed them into the sea. Their family erected a memorial stone on the Brigg in memory of the couple, intended to warn others. This stone is now on display in Filey Museum. At the same spot, fifty years later, Albert Shakesby, a primitive Methodist evangelist, rescued a young lady visitor who said, 'I owe my life to him; he is a brave man.'

Agony Point shows the plaque erected by the Paget family to warn others of the dangers of the Brigg.

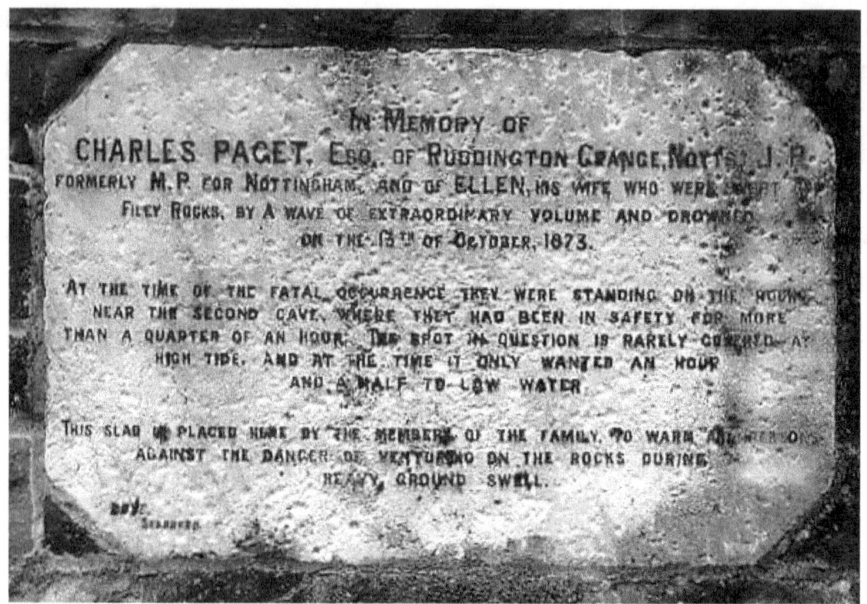

Searching for the bodies in 1873

The Wreck of The Chilean 1894

The Wreck of The Chilean 1894

In 1894, a steamer named the *Chilean*, a new vessel belonging to The Grimsby Incorporated Box Fishing Company (Limited), was on its way back to its home port of Grimsby after a journey to Iceland. It was just heading into Filey Bay when dense fog prevented the steamer's Captain Little from knowing his exact whereabouts (there had been problems with the vessel's compass instrument). Captain Little ordered the full engineer's steam astern but found that the ship would not come off. He blew the whistle with one long blast until he had no choice but to save himself and his crew.

Twenty minutes later, the vessel crashed into Filey Brigg. The ship was steering southeast, and a light breeze blew in the same direction. Captain Little sent a warning of the dangers that lay ahead to the steam-trawler that was following his pilotage, averting a second disaster. The captain then grabbed a life jacket and told his crew to take it to the rigging, but only he and four others did. Four hours passed before a trawler came and saved them.

Six of the other crew who attempted to launch the small boat were washed away by the heavy waves crashing over the ship and onto the Brigg. A man's body was found on the deck, taken to T'Oard' Ship Inn, Queen Street, and later identified as Charles Barker from Scarborough.

A few feet away from the Brigg, a well-known bell buoy would toll when the vessel struck, but the noise of the breakers prevented any warning to the steamer. The gun at Flamborough Head, which is sounded every five minutes in foggy weather, also failed to warn the steamer of its proximity to the rocks.

Credit Ian Nisbet

Filey Brigg Offered For Sale

Scarborough Mercury 1931

Today, it is inconceivable to consider that the Brigg was once in private ownership. However, it only became freely accessible to the public in 1955. Before this, the Lord of The Manor of Filey and owner of Hunmanby Hall and Estates owned the Brigg. He kept manorial rites over it and held a part of the foreshore.

Ancient manorial rights in England date back to the Norman Conquest. Whereby manorialism was characterised by vesting powers in the Lord of the manor. William, the Conqueror to Gilbert de Gant, the Manor of

Hunmanby, gave the authority over Filey to Hunmanby, becoming one of the most powerful manors in the North of England. Gilbert's son William founded Bridlington Priory, built with some of the stone from Filey Brigg.

The manor changed hands several times throughout the centuries but kept its manorial importance until the nineteenth century. Then the hereditary Lord of the Manor sold the estate to the High Sheriff of Yorkshire, Sir Dennis Readett Dennis-Bayley, a Nottinghamshire Coal Mine owner, who in 1925/6 sold the land piece by piece to his tenants. As the owner of Hunmanby estates, and thus The Lord of the Manor of Filey, he may exercise his ancient manorial rights and perform a 'Patrol of the Brigg', a ceremony performed every three or four years and for many years previously. This rite comprised dragging a net around the sea-line of the Brigg and gathering fish to distribute among the local people. An assistant to the Lord would then mount a horse and ride over the Brigg as far as the low-water mark.

Sir Readett-Bayley took his role seriously. In 1930, he wrote to Filey Urban District Council to complain about 'unauthorised people using the sands on his land to exercise their horses (riding school) and that he intended to prevent them!' The council replied that this was not a matter where they could intervene. Sir Readett-Bayley also pointed out that the adjoining landowners owned the property up to the high-water mark. The board of trade and Filey Town council have certain rights, and the uninterrupted usage by the public was a factor to be considered.

In March 1931, an advertisement appeared in the press that Sir Readett-Bayley had offered Filey Brigg for sale. The sale included part of the foreshore and manorial and mineral rights. The announcement (Yorkshire Post/Leeds Intelligencer/Scarborough Mercury) stipulated that the Lord of the Manor would consider selling the Brigg only or The Brigg with the foreshore and mineral rights.

Perhaps Sir Readett-Bayley was calling Filey Urban District Council's bluff. Still, they responded stating that 'if the Brigg were to pass into private ownership-and an attempt made to exclude the public then the council would have a duty to the public to intervene and safeguard any rights, with a passage over any private properties.

However, before the onslaught of the second world war, a proposal was put forward to Filey Urban District Council by a Leeds-based syndicate for substantial development of 320 acres of land belonging to The Church Cliff Estate, between the Brigg and Church Ravine and beyond. Mr Tom Smith, the owner of Church Cliff Farm, discussed the intentions of the syndicate, which were to build a first-class housing estate, shops, a large hotel, a concert hall and a cinema. He also showed that included in this sale was Carr Naze. However, it could comprise the Brigg and part of the Foreshore (still in the ownership of Sir Readett-Bayley), subject to negotiation. The proposal included developing this area. The syndicate would provide a lift from the cliffs to the beach. They would also build a promenade from the beach to the Brigg.

Mr W Bramham, another syndicate member, stated that pending a few minor details, the purchase was completed and proposed that the priority was to build three-hundred quality houses on the land, expressing that a development of this type would be beneficial for Filey as a town. Filey Urban District Council approved all the plans and favoured the development, but the purchase did not go ahead until after the war.

FILEY, YORKSHIRE.

JOSEPH CUNDALL and SONS will offer for Sale by Auction, unless previously sold by Private Treaty, and subject to Conditions of Sale, at the THREE TUNS HOTEL, FILEY, on FRIDAY, 29th SEPTEMBER, at 3 p.m. precisely.

The VALUABLE FREEHOLD BUILDING and AGRICULTURAL PROPERTY known as

CHURCH CLIFF FARM,

FILEY, containing 320.439 ACRES or thereabouts, situate in a commanding position adjoining the Ravine and the shore of Filey Bay, and lying in a ring fence extending to Filey Brigg, together with the SUPERIOR RESIDENCE and EXTENSIVE RANGE OF FARM BUILDINGS

The property has a sea frontage of about two miles and long road frontage to the Scarborough Road, and it is believed that future development will include a substantial part if not the whole of the land, a good deal of which is potential building land.

Further particulars and Permission to View may be obtained from the Auctioneers, Sherburn, Malton, Yorks.; or from the Solicitors, Messrs. LAMBERT and PARKINSON, Bridlington and Filey.

Advert Yorkshire Post/Leeds Intelligencer 1944

In 1945, following the war, Church Cliff Farm sold 320,439 acres of land for £24,500 to a Mr Taylor of Driffield. When asked what he thought would be best to do with this substantial amount of land, Mr Taylor responded he had bought the land specifically for speculation. His foremost intention was to make money. However, he liked Filey and wanted the best development possible for the town. However, he was shocked that the council did not favour his plans and objected to him building houses within 100 feet of the coastline with spectacular views.

Although the council had agreed to planning approval before the war, the new Town and Country Planning Act empowered authorities to revoke previous development approvals and query decisions. Filey Urban District Council took advantage of this act and revoked their authorisation to the earlier agreed plans.

Mr Taylor was not at all happy with this decision. He argued the matter at an enquiry, stating he would consider offering the land to the Council on Carr Naze to build a war memorial. However, if they wanted more land, they would have to buy it from him at a reasonable price of less than £5,000.

Filey Council and Mr Taylor were at loggerheads, with neither side talking to each other only via solicitors.

Wisely, the parties compromised and decided in favour of the Town Council. The ministry refused Mr Taylor's planning application not to allow building near Carr Naze in the northeast of the town in the town's public interest. Revised plans for a much-needed housing estate were submitted and agreed upon by each party.

Five years later, Filey Councillor Kenneth Henderson announced in the Yorkshire Post/Leeds Intelligencer under the Public Health Act 1875. It had started private negotiations with representatives of the late Sir Henry Readett-Bayley (he died in 1940) to purchase the Brigg for the benefit of the people of Filey. They planned to keep the Brigg for public use. The council purchased the Brigg for the sum of two-hundred and fifty pounds. Thus, the Brigg was not in private ownership for the first time. The council now owned all their sea-boundaries districts and has been enjoyed freely by many people.

A Cafe on The Brigg

The Original Cafe on the Brigg

Awelcome sight for thirsty travellers was a cafe on the Brigg. Unfortunately, in March 1906, a severe storm ravaged the town of Filey, and the cafe and its contents were completely swept away by the high tides. The café, a large brick and wood structure at the Brigg's shore end, was a visitor's favourite. The café contained many chairs, tables, stoves, freezers and crockery. Mr T. N Gray of Filey had only recently purchased the café.

The Vicar of Filey Canon Cooper started a charity to replace the cafe because Mr Gray had lost his entire life savings.

The New Cafe was built after the Storm of 1906

Spittal Rocks

On the south side of Filey Brigg is a rocky peninsula known as The Spittals. There has been speculation about whether this is a natural or a man-made structure. Some say this spectacular structure remains an ancient Roman road or harbour. In contrast, others say it was constructed purposely to transport stone across the Brigg to build Bridlington Priory. This magnificent structure is 600 meters long and thirty paces wide. Records show fishermen have seen old iron mooring rings exposed at the shallow tide. Also, when the tide is very low, some rare anemones can be found in the crevices beneath the layers of rocks near the water's edge. The Spittals are not accessible except at spring tides when they offer a rich reward for the naturalist seeking treasure.

Monsters and Dragons

In 1857, Mr Ruddock of Filey discovered 'A Monster of the Deep', an oceanic creature washed up on the beach a half-mile from the sea-wall parade. This 'monster' was 33 feet long, had fins and ten feet, and weighed twenty pounds. Later in 1934, several sightings of monsters spotted off Filey Brigg created a sensation. Reports varied, some saying that the beast had 'eyes like saucers, humps, scales and a large body.' One report stated that a man walking on the Brigg had seen a monster in the sea with a small head and many humps. Further investigation found that the beast was a school of porpoises swimming in a row.

On another occasion, fishermen thought they saw a giant sea monster two miles offshore. They rushed to get a better view, finding a large seal basking on the rocks.

Reports continue of strange 'monsters' seen in the sea around Filey. Who knows, perhaps one day, the real monster may reveal itself.

Spa Well

Spa Well, the Summer House in the background

During the early nineteenth century, taking the waters was a Victorian passion around the country. Spa towns flourished, and Filey was no exception and offered its contribution to the town's development as a seaside resort by supplying visitors with a stimulating health cure as 'healing spa water.'

The spa, which no longer exists, was centred upon a small spring alleged to have healing qualities. It was on the north side of Carr-Naze and was not a place to seek for the faint-hearted, as it was situated close to the edge, and a step in the wrong direction could have fatal consequences. To reach the spa, visitors had to walk about a quarter of a mile from North Coble Landing across the beach, then onto the Brigg, where steps led to the Spa Well. It is here where visitors first encounter the running water. This projection was aptly named 'agony point'. In 1844, Dr William Cortis persuaded the then-owner of the land, Miss Brooke of Selby, to open the Spa to the public. Before his intervention, the Spa was virtually unknown. The area was full of weeds and rubbish and challenging to find. Dr Cortis suggested that the well be more accessible, with an excellent road.

Miss Brooke took the doctor's advice and erected a summerhouse allowing visitors to take in the views through the season. For some years, Miss Brooke collected subscriptions from the public, which she used to employ an attendant to dispense the water. Two eminent specialists, Professor Fyfe of Edinburgh and Mr West of Leeds, had analysed the water and found that it possessed valuable medicinal properties. An unknown visitor dedicated this poem to Miss Brooke to thank her for making the 'Spa Well' available to the public.

On the Renovation of Filey Spa

A blessing meets us here on this hill

Gives from its brow a trickling rill

With healing virtues rife,

In rude neglect, t'was long concealed

Now, to the public gaze, it revealed

Its waters oft' may prove a well of life

Thanks to the lady who kindly thought

I was to such a pleasing beauty wrought

The birthplace of this spring

She wound a pathway to this spot

She rear'd the cool umbrageous grot

Where grandeur hovers around on breezy wing

But let our highest thanks be given

To him, who from his throne in heaven

Regards, all human wants

He bids to elevate the soul

The mighty waves of the ocean roll

And for the body's health, this well-spring grants

The notorious Dr Edward William Pritchard reiterated this claim in his book *A Guide to Filey*, claiming that 'taking the waters has significant gains for your health. The water's medicinal values are efficacious in treating dyspepsia, scrofula, and nervous diseases.' He also claimed that the water contained magnesium, calcium and soda, with a small quantity of iron, iodine and bromine. 'Which are all beneficial for one's health and help maintain the body's equilibrium.' However, later there were claims that the health-giving properties of the waters were dubious and exaggerated. There was no proof that the spa waters were a cure for chronic rheumatism and a miraculous treatment for most general nervous conditions, together with ailments of a 'scrupulous or scorbutic nature'.

Miss Brook died in 1869, and the property changed hands. A dispute arose over access to the right of way to the Spa on privately owned land. This dispute resulted in the Spa's closure. The Spa, like many others around the country, fell from favour with more trusted and readily available medicines. After the closure of the Spa, the new owner discovered Victorian graffiti inscribed on the boarding.

Though boarded up

It still flows out

Drink for dyspepsia

Or for gout

In 1951, for the Festival of Britain. A Filey local History Group spent time and effort restoring the site. Unfortunately, due to coastal erosion. All that remained of the Spa has since slipped down the cliff and into the sea.

John Paul Jones and the Battle of the Bonhomme Richard

The Battle of *The Bonhomme Richard* was fought off Filey Bay in September 1779. For generations been described as a memorable and intense battle, resulting in the events still being discussed over two centuries later. The story's central character is Captain John Paul Jones, a man who has attracted the attention of two continents and who, in his brief career, has received eternal fame among the heroes of the world.

John Paul (he added the Jones later, in tribute to his close friend and active American Revolutionary leader Willie Jones) was born of humble origin on the 6th of July 1747 in Kirkcudbrightshire, Scotland. John Paul was the fourth child of seven children. John Paul Snr's father was a gardener for the Earl of Selkirk. His mother was Jean McDuff (part of the McDuff clan). Neither of his parents registered their son's birth.

Living close to the sea, Jones soon developed a spirit for seafaring and adventure. At twelve, the young John Paul ran away to sea and signed up for a seven-year seaman's apprenticeship. His first voyage took him to Barbados and Fredericksburg in Virginia, where he learned navigation.

He soon adopted America as his native country and considered England, his enemy. In 1768, he took part in transporting slaves in ships unfit for humans. He soon quit making his fortune as a merchant seaman. Soon after, he faced arrest for the alleged murder of a crew member who he ordered to be flogged. Jones later produced evidence to show that the man died not from his wounds but from yellow fever whilst on another ship.

Cleared of those charges, he was embroiled in a second scandal when he ran his broadsword through a sailor. According to the letter written years later to Benjamin Franklin, Jones had to defend himself against the ringleader of a mutinous crew while in the West Indies. He noted this incident was the 'greatest misfortune of my life.' By his account, he immediately rowed ashore to the island of Tobago to turn himself into the Justice of the Peace. However, his friends advised him to leave his accumulated fortune behind him and flee to America, which he did before there was time for him to stand trial.

John Paul was still poor and obscure when he arrived in the colonies in 1774, taking the name John Paul Jones. Fortunately for him, he was in the right place at the right time and quickly climbed the ranks within America's plight for independence. He wrote to Joseph Hewes (who signed America's Declaration of Independence) to ask him personally for a naval appointment. In December 1775, he was appointed a First Lieutenant in the Navy.

The American War of Independence was an armed conflict between Great Britain and thirteen of its former North American colonies. From 1775 to 1783, the conflict with the Declaration of Independence on 4th July 1776. Relations between Britain and her American colonies had deteriorated following a British attempt to make the colonies contribute to the cost of their defence. Those opposing this wanted to break free from constraints imposed by the British aristocracy. Fundamentalists and radical politicians like Sam Adams and Paul Revere encouraged a break with Britain, while others hoped this drastic action would be avoided.

The descent into armed conflict between patriot (anti-British) and loyalist (pro-British) sympathisers was gradual. Events such as the Boston Massacre of 1770, when British troops fired on a mob that had attacked a British sentry outside Boston's State House, and the Boston 'tea party' of 1773, when British tea was thrown into the harbour, were key turning points. The takeover of the colonial militias was less pronounced. Initially, Americans formed the militia to defend against the French and the Native Americans. Officers ran these units in sympathy with the American patriots/rebels rather than soldiers sympathising with pro-British loyalists. After initial clashes in 1775, the British landed thirty thousand troops near New York under General Howe in the summer of 1776. The city was taken, and the war began.

Jones was appointed 1st lieutenant of the 24-gun frigate USS *Alfred*, a small, converted merchantman in the newly founded Continental Navy, on 7th December 1775. The flagship of Commodore Hopkins. He was the first to raise 'The Grand Union Liberty Flag' on this ship. There is also controversy about whether this was the stars and stripes flag or the famous yellow silk banner with a rattlesnake and perhaps a pine tree emblazoned upon it with the significant legend. 'Don't tread on me!'

Credit US Bonhomme Richard (January 2017)

He later captained '*The Ranger*', and in 1778, Jones and his crew crossed the Solway Frith from Whitehaven to Scotland, hoping to take for ransom the Earl of Selkirk (the very man his father had worked for). Jones intended to kidnap and exchange him for American sailors *impressed* into the Royal Navy. However, The Earl was not at home, only the countess and her young family. Instead, Jones and his crew made off with the silverware from the estate. Jones continued his journey raiding Whitehaven on the northwest coast of England and seeing action in Ireland and Scotland (earning the reputation of a 'pirate' in Britain) before taking charge of the 44-gun USS *Bonhomme Richard* in 1779.

The *Bonhomme Richard* was an aged East Indiaman. Initially built in 1765, it was formerly named *Duc de Duras*, a merchant ship built for the French East India Co for service between France and the Orient. The vessel was placed at the disposal of John Paul Jones on 4th February 1779 by King Louis XVI of France because of a loan to the United States by French shipping magnate Jacques-Donatien Le Ray de Chaumont, who historians consider being the 'Father of the American Revolution. To compliment Benjamin Franklin's almanack, '*Poor Richard,*' the ship was renamed *The Bonhomme Richard* (Good Man Richard). When Jones took her command, the vessel had already had four gruelling voyages to the Far East and back. This old vessel was not the type of ship Jones was expecting, having already declared, 'I will have no connection with any ship that does not sail fast, for I intend to go in harm's way.'

Initially, the *Duc de Duras* was designed as a two-decker with 32 guns, with two-gun decks which ran from bow to stern. However, Jones later adapted the ship to suit his needs. Jones hand-picked his crew, and a letter in *The London Chronicle* of the 28th of September 1779 states that most of Jones' crew were English and Irish, many taken out of Brest and St. Malo prisons. Prisoners were offered the liberty of serving on Jones' fleet. However, they were treated as prisoners whilst on board. The article quotes: 'There were few Americans, some French and some neutrals, such as Dutch and Germans'.

Captain Richard Pearson took a commission of *The Serapis* on 8th March 1779. Captain Richard Pearson was born in Appleby, Westmoreland, in 1731. He entered the Navy in 1745, aged fourteen. Pearson was a lieutenant during the Seven Years' War, where he was very successful but badly wounded in the conflict. Pearson finally received his commission as captain in January 1773. *The Serapis* was launched from Deptford Dockyard in March of the same year. Named after the Greek God of fertility and the afterlife, *The Serapis* is described as having been an exceedingly fine ship with good sailing properties. *The Serapis* was rated a 44-gun ship and mounted her guns on two complete decks. The present complement of the class was a trained man-of-war's crew of two hundred and eighty-five men.

The Serapis at Sea

Jones' orders were simple. He would 'burn, sink or destroy all.' *The Bonhomme Richard*, together with four smaller vessels, *The Alliance*, *The Pallas*, *The Cerf*, and *The Vengeance*, of which only *The Alliance* and *The Cerf*

were adequately fitted for war, set sail from L'Orient on 19th June 1779, striking terror on their journey.

On 23rd September 1779, *The Serapis* and *The Countess of Scarborough* took anchor under Scarborough Castle. Captain Pearson received intelligence that Jones and his American convoy were in Burlington Bay (Bridlington), a few leagues windward. The English ships departed, watching for the American convoy and its notorious Commodore John Paul Jones. Around six in the evening, it was all hands to quarters as four vessels came into sight. *The Serapis* signalled to The Countess of Scarborough to stay close to their stern whilst hoisting the English colours on both ships.

The evening wind was slight as the American ships came up slowly. As a decoy, Captain Pearson instructed that the ports in the lower deck were to be down. However, the enemy was far too cunning and soon saw through this. At about seven-thirty, the enemy ships bore close and hoisted American colours, but it was so dark that they were presumed to be the colours of St. George.

The orders were given that on pain of death, not to fire. To be sure, Captain Pearson hailed her and believed the response to be '*Princess Amelia.*' He called again with the warning: 'If you do not tell us whence you came, we will fire you (now they were very close, within half a pistol shot, but it was too dark to recognise their colours). Suddenly, a flash of gunfire was on one of the lower decks. *The Serapis* responded instantaneously by giving them a broadside. Initially, *The Serapis* had superior firepower. However, John Paul Jones fought at close range to overcome his disadvantage. The ships were so close that the nozzles of the guns touched as the vessels rolled on heavy seas. There was no time to be lost. The enemy was all too close, every shot told.

The crew had no choice but to haul the dead and wounded from the guns, fire, and load simultaneously.

A vast crowd had gathered on the cliffs and shore to watch the battle in the rising moon's light. Some gunfire was so near that a few cannonballs grazed Flamborough's white cliffs. Firing continued for the next two hours, with many deaths on both sides and people jumping ships to save themselves. Jones carried away the jibboom from *The Serapis* (to ensure they would not sail off too far). *The Bonhomme Richard's* bow and *The Serapis* touched, and shots were fired as fast as they could each raise guns.

Gradually, *The Serapis* shot away from the entire side of *The Bonhomme Richard,* which was riddled like a sieve, causing the ship to take in several feet of water in the hold. Her rotten sides were almost blown out to starboard and port by the batteries of *The Serapis.* Captain Pearson was a brave man, but he was no match for the indomitable personality of the American Commander. After several hours of fighting, he asked Jones if he wanted to strike (surrender), to which Jones famously replied, 'I have not yet begun to fight.' Reports state that, unlike the honourable Captain Pearson, Jones would have sunk the ship, men, and himself, before he would have 'struck.' When told that *The Bonhomme Richard* was falling, Jones said, 'let her sink and be damned. She cannot be in a better place than alongside an English man-of-war!' Some of Jones' crew cried out, 'we have struck', and *The Serapis* Boatswain went on board *The Bonhomme Richard* to take possession of her. He was met with a Frenchman's small sword in his groin and another through his brain. He fell back onto *The Serapis,* where he died instantly.

The Bonhomme Richard's damaged gun decks could barely fight. It was a terrible scene. There were dead lying on the living. There were men without arms and legs, many bleeding to death as there were no dressings. Two of the three doctors were dead. Besides, there were no dressings left. Yet, with Jones' leadership and determination, the remaining crew fought through the night.

Gun Deck onboard The Bonhomme Richard

As the water rose in *The Bonhomme Richard*, fear set into the mind of John Burbank, her master-at-arms. He took pity on the crying prisoners trapped in the hole with water rising around them. Without orders, Burbank opened hatches and released the British prisoners caught in previous actions. Jones was furious and put them to work manning the sinking ship's water pumps. These prisoners were terrified but grateful to have been set free. They could have easily tipped the balance against the Americans, and they could have all bolted and jumped ship, shot Jones or thrown him overboard, but most of them stayed put. Perhaps they were more concerned with saving themselves from imminent drowning or being shot on the spot. Still, they became integral to the subsequent American victory because of their actions.

However, a few did escape taking advantage of the confusion and made their escape to Filey, where they were taken prisoner before Humphrey Osbaldeston, Hunmanby.

Conflict on The Bonhomme Richard

Once again, Captain Pearson called Jones to strike, or you must infallibly sink to the bottom. Jones replied, 'I may sink, but I'll be damned if I strike!' One of Jones' crew attempted to strike the colours, but Jones turned around and shot him dead. Another two attempted and suffered the same fate. Jones expected a mutiny as the ship sank when one of Jones' squadron immediately came to his assistance turning the tables on *The Serapis*. *The Bonhomme Richard* was in such a grave way. The rudder was gone, the stern frame and stanchions were cut away, the timbers of the lower deck from the mainmast to stern were mangled beyond recognition, and dying men were lying in pools of blood and groaning piteously. The ship was burning in several places, and the water in the hold rose steadily. Realising that *The Bonhomme Richard* was sinking and the seriousness of the situation, Jones still fought until the mizzenmast of *The Serapis* went by the board. At that point, Captain Pearson called for quarter. Jones then ordered a boarding crew onto *The Serapis* and, against all odds, captured *The Serapis* and its crew, where they triumphantly raised their country's colours. *The Countess of Scarborough* suffered a similar fate as she surrendered to *The Pallas* and *The Alliance*.

Many men lost their lives on both sides of the conflict. Here is an account of the ship's men and guns before engagement.

The American's Capt. Jones	Guns	Men
Bonhomme Richard - Jones	44	380
Pallas-Cpt Cottineau	32	320
Alliance-Cpt Landais	36	300

Vengeance	12	100
TOTAL	**124**	**1100**
THE ENGLISH	Guns	Men
The Serapis-Cpt-Pearson	44	285
The Countess of Scarborough	20	100
TOTAL	**64**	**385**

Therefore, Jones had three times more men than the English (715) and 60 more guns from the beginning of the battle.

Accounts from the time show that the loss of life on both sides was horrendous:

The Bonhomme Richard – 250 men killed and wounded.

The Pallas – 6 men and 1 lieutenant killed, with many wounded.

The Alliance – Nobody killed - 2 injured.

The English

The Serapis – 125 killed and wounded.

The Countess of Scarborough – 30 killed and wounded.

The total loss of life on both sides: is 411.

Two days later, between the hours of ten and eleven on the morning of 25th September, *The Bonhomme Richard* drifted towards Filey Bay, where she eventually sank, her flag flying as she went down. There was nothing of her left except her signal flag. John Paul Jones and his victorious crew and prizes sailed *The Serapis and The Countess of Scarborough* and Captain Pearson and his crew as hostages to Texel in the Netherlands, where Jones sought safe harbour and the ship received much-needed repairs.

The Serapis was the first British vessel ever captured by an American ship, causing British fears of an invasion and the possibility of a fleet being dispatched from across the Atlantic. The English were exasperated at the humiliation suffered by the total defeat of one of their best frigates.

Writing to the Dutch, British Ambassador Sir Joseph Yorke protested Jones' conduct on behalf of The King of England. Saying that '*The Serapis* and *The Countess of Scarborough* and their Captains and crew were attacked and taken by force by John Paul Jones, who had received no commission from his own country. Therefore, to the treaties and laws of war, he falls under the classification of Rebels and Pirates.' The Dutch did not agree to the Ambassador's request, stating that they would prefer to 'observe neutrality.' On 7th October, Jones left the ship and went to Amsterdam. Captain Pearson was kept as a hostage and finally released on 21st November 1779 in exchange for Captain Gustave Conyngham, whom the British were holding prisoner.

Captain Jones was not happy with John Burbank, the master-at-arms on The Bonhomme Richard, and placed him in irons to liberate prisoners during the conflict.

At a Court Martial for losing *The Serapis on* 3rd October 1870, Captain Pearson was honourably acquitted and knighted by the King of England for his services in this most famous battle. When Jones heard of this, he said: 'Never mind. If I meet him again, I'll make a Lord of him!' Captain Pearson died in 1806 at The Royal Naval Hospital in Greenwich, where he was Lieutenant Governor.

The Serapis were on loan to Benjamin Franklin to aid the American Revolution. The French ordered Captain Cottineau de Kerlogeun to take command of *The Serapis* in the Texel and bring her back to France. Subsequently, *The Serapis* was refitted for the French Navy and sent to assist in a campaign to wrest India from British rule under Captain

Roche. Roche proceeded to the French fort, Île Sainte-Marie, located off the northern coast of Madagascar. While Roche was ashore, a lieutenant and a subordinate went below deck to get the daily brandy ration for the sailors. While the men were 'cutting' the brandy's full strength with water, their lantern fell into the vat and set the spirit locker on fire. Attempts to extinguish the blaze failed, and after two-and-a-half hours, the flames burned through the locker walls and reached the powder magazine. An explosion blew out the stern, and the vessel sank.

Like the wreck of *The Bonhomme Richard*, The Serapis' whereabouts were unknown for many years. However, in November 1999, American nautical archaeologist Richard Swete and his associate Michael Tuttle discovered it. After many years of research and a systematic magnetometer survey of the harbour on Île Sainte-Marie, Swete and a team of archaeologists finally found the remains of *The Serapis*.

Despite being revered today, John Paul Jones received no promotion to a rank higher than captain in the American Navy. Strangely enough, he became an admiral in 1788. However, ironically, it was in Russia's Black Sea fleet at the invitation of Empress Catherine II. He was also appointed US Consul to Algiers in 1792, but he never got the chance to take up this position, as on 18th July 1792, John Paul Jones was found dead face down on his bed at his residence at Rue de Tournon Paris. He was forty-five years old. The cause of death was kidney failure.

John Paul Jones's burial occurred in Paris at the Saint Louis Cemetery, which belonged to the French royal family. France's revolutionary government sold the property and forgot the cemetery four years later. Jones's body was preserved in alcohol and interred in a lead coffin in case the United States decided to claim his remains. They might be more readily identifiable.' After a lengthy search, Jones' body was taken back to America.

On 24th April 1906, the Americans brought Jones' coffin to Bancroft Hall at the United States Naval Academy, Annapolis, Maryland. On 26th January 1913, the captain's remains were finally re-interred in a magnificent bronze and marble casket at the Naval Academy Chapel in Annapolis. Americans consider John Paul Jones to be the father of the father of the American Navy.

To this day, the search for the wreckage of *The Bonhomme Richard* continues. Recovering this salvage cannot be an easy task. After all, this was an ageing ship (14 years old before it sank) that had been at the bottom of the sea for over two hundred and thirty years. It was constructed of timber and was severely damaged and on fire before sinking. If located, it would be an incredible find for the Americans and boost tourism in the area, putting Filey and the Yorkshire Coast firmly at the centre of American history and an integral part of its fight for Independence.

The house in Paris where John Paul Jones died

Sir Captain Richard Pearson

In a letter dated 14th October 1779, Captain Richard Pearson gives his account of the battle, in which he states:

'On my going on board *The Bonhomme Richard*. I found her in great distress. Her quarters and counter on the lower deck entirely drove in. The whole of her lower decks dismounted. She was also on fire in two places, with six or seven feet of water in her hold, which increased throughout the night and the next day. Eventually, the crew had to quit her, and she sank, with many wounded people on board her. She had 306 men killed and wounded in action. I am incredibly sorry for losing his majesty's ship that I had the honour to command. I also flatter myself, hoping to convince the Lordship that she has not been given away. Every exertion possible was used to defend her.

Two essential pieces of service to our country have arisen from her. The one is wholly over setting the crews of this flying squadron. The other refers to the whole of a valuable convoy into the hands of the enemy, which I believe would have been the case had I acted other than the way I did.'

Filey Harbour of Refuge

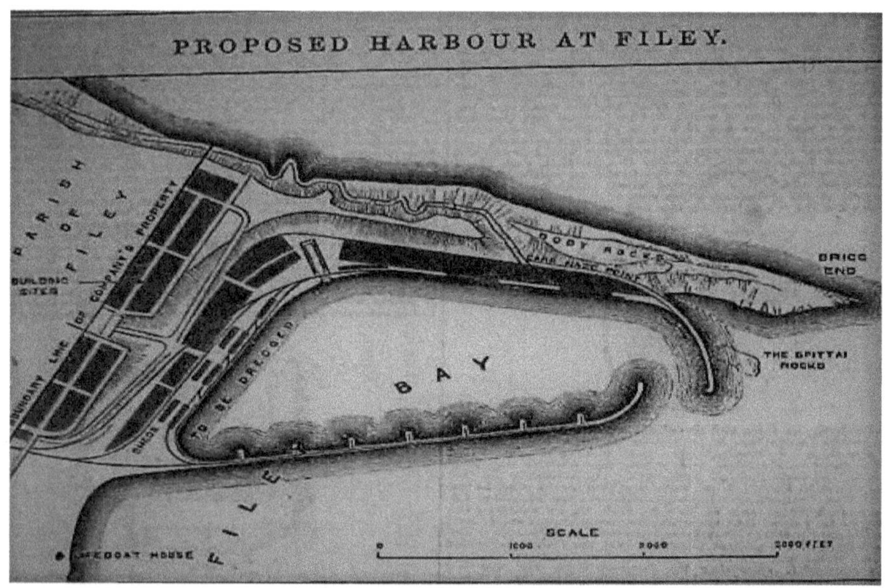

For many years, there had been proposals for building a Harbour in Filey. The reasons were threefold. First, many lives were lost at sea each year because of adverse weather, and a harbour would be a safe place of refuge for sailing ships. Second, the import and export of general cargo, and third, for a place to land fish and maintain vessels.

In 1858, Prime minister Viscount Palmerston set up a Royal select committee to report on the most helpful places for forming Harbours of Refuge along the coast of England. Subsequently, a panel of seven 'experts', including sea captains and Royal Navy engineers, were elected who were expected to be 'competent and impartial'. The sites in question were Wick, Peterhead, The Tyne, Hartlepool, St. Ives, Padstow, Isle of Man and Filey.

To support a harbour at Filey, Civil Engineer John Coode presented detailed proposals to Parliament with over 3,000 signatures from masters, mates, and seamen regarding building a harbour of refuge in Filey Bay. The petition recorded the estimated cost of the proposed harbour was £860,000.

'For centuries, southerly winds detained large vessels off Flamborough Head. Under these circumstances, vessels will constantly run in and bring up in the south part of Filey Bay, off Speeton and Bempton cliffs, where they will not uncommonly lay for a week. At one time, there were not less than 240 vessels anchored in the southern part of Filey Bay.'

In 1860, after a thorough investigation of all the proposed areas, the commission concluded that they could save approximately eight hundred lives and one million pounds in property on the country's shores each year. Therefore, the report earnestly recommended that Filey construct a national harbour of refuge entirely at the expense of the public. And for this purpose, the commission recommended the most extensive grant ever given to any public place in the three kingdoms of eight hundred thousand pounds.

The select committee submitted its report and advised that harbours around the coast were to be constructed and awarded the following grants:

Filey	£800,000
Hartlepool	£500,000
St. Ives	£400,000
The Tyne	£250,000

The Isle of Man	£140,000
Wick	£125,000
Peterhead	£100,000
Padstow	£40,000

Proposed Harbour of Refuge. Credit Stephen Eblet

However, despite the competent and impartial views of the select committee and Mr Coode's diligent research and the strength of his evidence supporting the project, nothing came of this scheme. The project was too expensive. In 1863 an eminent government officer said: 'It is not the duty of Government to care for the lives and property of merchant seamen.' Therefore, the government scheme deemed the expensive inquiry useless and abandoned.

Unperturbed, the town was determined to build a harbour. So, in December 1863, a company was formed to construct a pier and harbour on a smaller scale, as first recommended by the select committee. The company was called *The Filey Harbour Company*. Its distinguished directors were:

General Sir J M Frederick Smith (a part of the government select committee).

The Right Hon James Meek, Lord Mayor of York.

Henry Bentley, Ravine Hall, Filey.

George Beswick Esq, Muston Lodge, Filey.

C.W Faber, Director of Great Northern Railway.

J Kitson, Director Great Northern Railway.

George Salt Esq, Saltaire, Bradford.

John Unett Esq, Birmingham & Filey.

William S Cortis Esq, Engineer, Filey.

John Coode Esq, Engineer, London.

The company intended to build and maintain a harbour with piers, jetties, landing places, breakwaters, roads, and other conveniences. There would be a quay or a dock which would begin approximately 70 yards southward of a point on the western shore of Filey Bay to be called 'North Coble Landing' and extend 1130 yards in an easterly direction seaward. A breakwater begins near Carr Naze's eastern extremity point on the northern side of Filey Bay. It extends along Filey Brigg in an easterly direction along the 'Spittals' for 290 yards. The company intended to purchase land and get loans and mortgages as necessary. To fund the project, the company designed to levy tolls, rates and duties on vessels and boats using the harbour and impose an entrance fee for all persons wanting to enter the pier. Public subscription raised capital for a limited liability company, raising ten thousand pounds almost immediately. The share offer's total value was one hundred and fifty thousand pounds.

The proposal initially attracted local support, and the following year, a meeting was held at Taylor's Hotel on The Crescent. Mr John Unett, who favoured the scheme and believed that 'the harbour' would be of great national benefit, chaired the meeting. Mr Unett concluded his address by formally presenting the committee with a purse containing 160 guineas. However, by April 1884, no harbour had been constructed, and the shareholders could not raise the capital needed to take the project forward. In June 1884, the company was dissolved.

A less ambitious company named *Filey Fishery Harbour and Pier Co* was incorporated in May 1878. The chairman was Lord Claude John Hamilton. MP for Lynn and vice-president of The Great Northern Railway. Other directors included Lord Londesborough and Christopher Sykes MP. However, once again, this scheme never got off the ground.

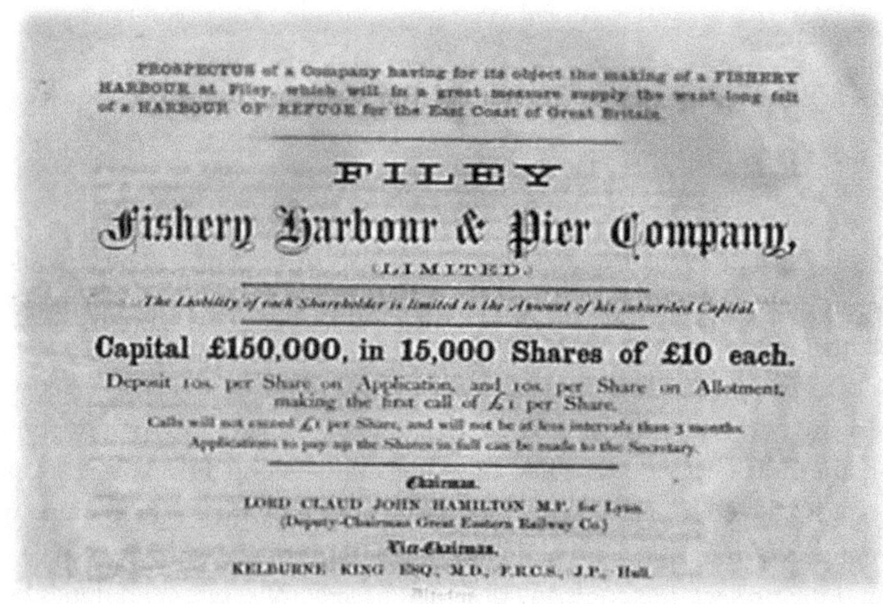

During this time, lack of government support was an issue. However, in January 1883, the government suggested that a harbour at Filey would be necessary for the country's defence and showed building it with convict labour at a cost in the region of £1,250,000. The other consideration was a Dover harbour, but Filey was the preferred location. However, Filey Brigg needed to be expanded to create a new harbour entrance, which would become an imposing fort to house a prison extending towards Reighton Sands. The proposed prison would have been constructed and homed 750 inmates and provided cheap labour for the scheme's building for twelve years.

The people of Filey were in an uproar, and the preservation of Filey's natural beauty was under threat. In the end, Langdon Prison was constructed on the white cliffs of Dover, although once more, a lack of Government support prevailed, and Dover did not get its promised harbour until the turn of the 20th century. Filey would not be what it is today if strong-minded people had not opposed this drastic plan to change its landscape.

Langdon Prison, Dover (Credit Dover Museum)

Filey's Churches

St Oswald's Filey Parish Church

As discussed in a previous chapter, during the Middle Ages, an original ancient Saxon church stood near the site of today's church dedicated to St Bartholomew. This was most likely in the field behind the present church. However, by the 16th century, this church was in ruins.

Tradition points to the possibility of a village in this vicinity, as some time back, mounds were discovered revealing buildings of different ages. These were possibly from the Beckwith and Buck families but could also be from an earlier period. A stone thought to belong to the choir or part of the chancel of the old Norman church was dug up in a field west of the gate of the goods yard of the railway station. (Now Tesco and Filey's workshops) For some time, this stone was stored in the backyard of the T'Oard Ship Inn on Queen Street. An altar approximately eighteen inches long was dug up a few years ago in the same field. No records remain of what happened to either of these artefacts.[3]

Artists' impression of the chancel found near the Railway Station.

St Oswald's, Filey's parish church, is a magnificent ancient Grade 1 listed building, built under the reign of Stephen and begun under the auspices of the Augustinian Canons at Bridlington, for whom Filey's benefactor

3 W.S. Cortis *An Historical and Descriptive Guide to Filey.* (1861)

Walter de Gant had founded a monastery. It is understood that the Bridlington Canons will have supplied St Oswald's with the clergy. Eventually, a settlement of Canons settled in Filey, who selected one to be their head whilst still depending on Bridlington.

 Sir Nikolaus Pevsner (renowned architect) describes the church as 'the finest church in the North-East corner of the East Riding's buildings of England.'

Still, people wonder why the church stands away from the town. Taking us back to when there was a 'North & South 'Fieling'.'

The ravine separates the original village of Filey, which stood on the north side under the rule of Pickering and Lythe in the North Riding. Years later, a village in the' East Riding' sprang up on the south side with a market. Therefore, this part of the town grew as it came under the wapentake of Dickering. According to Cole (1828), on the south side of the town was *Chapel Island,* upon which stood a *Chapel of Ease.* Unfortunately, no further information exists.

Nowadays, it is easy to cross the bridge and visit the church, but in times gone by, people went up and down the sides of the steep ravine by steps.

There would have been a rapid stream of water flowing and only a small narrow bridge to cross it (Gentleman's Magazine, 1805). However, this bridge was destroyed by a great storm in 1857 and replaced by a sturdier iron bridge. So, going to church cannot have been an easy task. Interestingly, while the ravine marks the boundary between North and South, it gives credence to a local saying when referring to a person's final journey: ' He's gaing acrass ti' North.'

Filey Parish Church 1832

The stone used for the church's construction probably came from Filey's ancient quarry, located somewhere on the North Cliff. This quarry also provided Bridlington Priory's building stone on Walter de Gant's orders. It is also likely that stone from the original late 12th-century Saxon church was used with stone from early houses in the same area. Information also suggests that the stone from the original church could have come from the Roman signal station in this area. Unfortunately, it is unlikely that this can be confirmed.

Like many other churches in the country, Filey adopted St Oswald as their patron saint. King Oswald was the first king to bring together church and state since Roman times, and he is renowned for uniting Britain and converting the English to Christianity. The tradition of state-backed religion started at Lindisfarne with the first monastery. This period, known as 'The Golden Age of Lindisfarne', was primarily responsible for some key moments in British history, from the Crusades to the Reformation.

With the support of King Oswald, this monastery set up a school to teach reading and writing (in Latin). The monastery trained young boys as missionaries who spread the Gospel in England. Women were also encouraged to give themselves to God and become nuns. The Lindisfarne Gospels are prime examples of creative Christian skills which survive today.

King Oswald was a popular king who ruled for eight years before being defeated and dismembered in the battle of Maserfield between 641 and 642. After his death, the brave, pious king was canonised and venerated in England and Europe as a saint. King Oswald's legacy continued throughout the mediaeval period, as his bones and ashes were scattered around Europe and treasured by religious communities.

The writer, J.R.R Tolkien, took inspiration from St Oswald (he was once a professor of Anglo-Saxon History at Oxford University) for his character of Aragorn in his novel 'The Hobbit. Aragorn joins Frodo the Hobbit on a quest to destroy the King before returning to Gondor, the land of his ancestry, thus claiming his rightful place as king. Like the real King Oswald. Historians suggest that King Oswald bears more than a striking resemblance to the hero in the Anglo-Saxon cultural achievement. He was the source of the inspiration behind the epic poem Beowulf.

The church's original design was early gothic, and it had a nave only with a West Tower. There is space in the west wall for a staircase, and a window remains visible only from the outside. This west tower's construction stopped following the Southwest Pier's failure. A stone altar was found on the chancel floor early in the 20th century, dating back to the 1500s, probably during the Reformation. A small cross can be seen on each of the four corners, symbolling where the nails pierced Christ's hands and feet when nailed to the cross, and a large one in the centre of the altar represents where the sword pierced His side. Maybe this altar possibly belonged to the old original Saxon church.

High in the tower are three musical bells, which bear the following inscriptions:

1st Bell

Fiat Voluntas Pater Omnipotence 1682

2nd Bell

Sole Deo Gloria Pax Hominibus 1700

3rd Bell

Gloria Deo In Excelsis 1675

(These inscriptions are transcribed from the original)

The church has undergone much restoration through the centuries, and a substantial restoration occurred again in 1839, with contributions from Henry Bentley Esq (Ravine Villa) and several smaller subscribers. Joseph Stocks Esq donated a valuable communion plate, and Mrs Bentley of Ravine Hall presented a new organ to the church.

A further partial repair happened in 1885. The plaster was removed from the walls, revealing the original stonework for the first time in 700 years. Unfortunately, the walls were white-washed, and many ancient features were destroyed. A fire in 1908 almost obliterated the church. Fortunately, a choir boy spotted the fire and raised the alarm. The fire caused severe damage to the organ. Unfortunately, it was beyond repair and replaced by the present organ built on the side of the chancel. However, the church needed a new roof.

Once again, damage occurred to the church during the Dogger-Bank Earthquake of 1932, measured at 6.1 on the Richter scale. The church's spire was damaged.

Methodists-Wesleyan & Primitive

Compared to many other towns throughout the country, Methodism came relatively late to Filey. The earliest branch meeting of the Wesleyan Methodist church was formed in 1811 at Back Lane (now Chapel Street). However, the chapel was not well attended, with only 15 members. To recruit more people, ministers preached through the streets, which did not go well with Filey residents, who often pelted the preachers with dried fish and anything else they had to hand. The ministers considered Filey a lost cause to include them in any branch of the Methodist society.

Filey people were stuck in their ways and were no pushovers. They were indifferent to change, especially regarding religion. Before 1823, Filey was a village of 'vice and wickedness. It was well known for its Sabbath-breaking, cockfighting, gambling, and swearing, and its people (both men and women) liked to get as drunk as possible. The Methodist movement considered the town and its people 'lost causes'.

This debauchery all changed in 1823 when a Methodist minister named John Oxtoby, or 'Praying Johnnie', came to town as he was affectionately known. He refused to give up on Filey. John was convinced that the people needed a vital religion to moralise them. John believed the fishermen needed faith to give them the strength to cope with storms and imminent danger. The women also needed religion to bear the strain of anxiety and comfort them in times of desolation.

John Oxtoby was born in 1767 near Pocklington. For about fifteen years, Oxtoby worked with the Wesleyan Methodists. He became an unofficial travelling itinerant, working mainly as an exhorter and prayer leader. In 1819, John met William Clowes (one founder of Primitive Methodism) and became his right-hand man. John joined the Primitive Methodist Connexion as he considered that many of the Primitive Methodists preachers were like-minded in their approach to mission.

John Wesley formed the Wesleyan Methodists. Wesley did not intend to find a new denomination, but historical circumstances and organisational genius conspired against his desire to remain in the Church of England. Wesley's followers first met in private home 'societies.' When these societies became too large for members to care for one another, Wesley organised 'classes,' each with eleven members and a leader. Classes met weekly to pray, read the Bible, discuss their spiritual lives, and collect charity money. Men and women met separately, but anyone could become a class leader.

John Wesley understood the importance of education; thus, Wesleyan day schools were opened around the country. The Wesleyans favoured more ornate buildings and concentrated on the needs of more affluent and influential urban classes. In contrast, the Primitive Methodists focused more on the role of laypeople and so focused on the rural poor.

In 1823, despite the misgivings of others, John refused to give up on Filey. The story goes that when walking up Muston Hill to convince the people of Filey to change their ways, he caught sight of Filey, fell to his knees, and prayed. He firmly believed that God would guide him. He rose from his knees, shouting, 'Filey is taken, Filey is taken!' A remarkable revival, with lasting results from that day on, laid the foundations of a substantial cause in Filey. Initially, meetings took place in barns and sheds. However, demand was so strong that the Primitive Methodists built a chapel called initially Bethesda, later known as The Albert Hall (now the Salvation Army).

Bethesda Chapel (The Albert Hall) Demolition 1974.

Credit Martin Douglas

In this religious revival, the Wesleyan society shared, as did St Oswald's parish church. Therefore, the villagers' morals rapidly improved. Religion wrought sobriety, thrift, better social manners, and domestic discord. It was the Filey fishermen who led the way in abandoning Sunday fishing. Ironically, the men who fished for six days had a bigger catch than those who worked for seven days.

By 1863, Filey had become a model fishing town. The Wesleyan Minister Rev. Edwin Day declared: 'This change was down to the Primitive Methodist Connexion.' Some prominent members helped shape its popularity, Mrs Gordon, the wife of the coastguard. Mrs Gordon was well-travelled, educated, and considered 'the queen of missionary collectors' who inspired others to do the same. A Mrs Jenkinson – known as 'Nan Jenk' – struck a deal with the fishermen whereby they would give the missionary a percentage of all the fish they caught above a certain quota on the condition that Mrs Jenkinson would pray for them when they were fishing. Mrs Jenkinson's husband, William, also converted and lived to see the 100th member of the society.

John Wyville (died 1866) was another of Filey's 'lost causes. That is until John Oxtoby placed his hands on his shoulders and said: 'Thou must be converted, for the Lord has great work for you to do!' Not long after, John joined the society, attended readings, cultivated his mind, and became an arduous and competent local preacher.

In 1865, simple but effective preaching was the success of Primitive Methodism. Hence, the chapel is known as the 'Ranter' chapel. Filey fishermen became staunch followers of the Primitive Methodist connexion and began spreading the word around Yorkshire and the north. To get their message across, they would spread the word of the Gospel in song, which was the beginning of The Filey fishermen's choir.

Primitive Methodism became such a popular Christian denomination in Filey that new premises were soon needed. Fundraising began, and legendary fish suppers were held to raise funds for a new chapel accommodating 900 people. In 1870, the foundation stone was laid on Union Street for a new chapel named 'Ebenezer'.

Ebenezer Chapel

Ebenezer 'Ranter' Chapel

Wesleyan Methodists, who had premises on the corner of Murray Street (later called The Victoria Rooms) and a day school (now Dixons Discount Warehouse), found their premises inadequate. A new church with a 90-foot spire and built-in gothic style on Union Street and Station Avenue junction. They were designed by Mr Petch of Scarborough, costing £4,700, and erected using a local tradesman. The church was called Trinity Methodist Church. The church opened in 1876, accommodating 600 people on the ground floor and 100 children in the lobby gallery. There was also a large schoolroom with four classrooms above it. A mysterious fire destroyed most of this building in 1918, and the church was rebuilt; it reopened its doors in 1923.

In the early 1970s, it was apparent that merging the two Methodist congregations would be advantageous, and Ebenezer closed its doors for the last time in May 1975 after 104 years of service. The two congregations were known as Filey Methodists from that day and continue today.

Filey Methodist Church

St Mary's Church and The Sisters of Charity of Our Lady of Evron

Perrine Thulard (1654-1735) was born in Chapelle au Riboul in Mayenne, France, on the 6th of November 1654. At twenty-five, Perrine became a widow. She dedicated her life to God and gave time to teaching young girls, caring for the sick and the welfare of those less fortunate. Hence, Perrine's work became well known, and other young girls became associated with her project, and together they formed 'The Society of Daughters of Charity.'

Following the French Third Republic's anti-clerical legislation, it became difficult for religious orders to continue teaching in France. Subsequently, the sisters extended their order to England. The sisters established their first congregation in Filey in 1904. The Roman Catholics did not have a presence in the town. Thus, Father Eugene Roulin, a French Benedictine monk, was appointed by Ampleforth Abbey as chaplain to the sisters, and he became the town's first resident Roman Catholic Priest. Father Roulin was a very charismatic character and oversaw the architecture and design of the St Mary's Catholic Church building in Brooklands. Father Roulin and the nuns were a welcome and much-respected sight in Filey. Their presence increased Catholic visitors to the town and was a welcome boost for local businesses.

The nuns purchased the property at 1 & 2 South Crescent Villas, and the convent school opened on the Feast of the Sacred Heart in 1909. Besides the boarding school. The sisters ran a parish school known as 'The Villa School' because the school was at the foot of the cliffs at the Villa Ambrosia (now 21, The Beach). This 'Free' school was devoted to the less well-off children in Filey and fulfilled the initial mission of the sisters of Evron.

In 1913, the convent advertised adult education classes for anyone over twelve. The sisters offered courses in 'cutting out, sewing and mending every weekday evening at the cost of threepence per session. Fancy needlework costs an additional three pence.

Despite the First World War, the school continued to expand, and by 1921 there were 102 pupils, 22 of which were full-time boarders, increasing to 70 boarders by 1950. While most pupils were girls, the school taught boys up to eight, including Charles Laughton, a famous actor and Hollywood film star. The convent-educated other famous people, including Lana Bowen-Woods, who became a very successful crime writer named Sara Woods. Like most schools of this era, the regime was strict, but the education was thorough and long-lasting.

Over the next thirty years, the increase in pupils caused expansion, including a large dormitory for younger boarders, a gymnasium, and cloakrooms. An average school day started at 7.30 with breakfast, then Mass in the Convent Chapel, perhaps a hockey game on the beach, or the curriculum lessons, including French taught by the native-speaking nuns. A supper of bread, cocoa, prayers, and bed followed homework.

The school uniform was easily recognisable, and the girls were familiar with Filey in the winter, dressed in their black felt or velour hats, navy blue coats, and dresses. The summer costume was navy blue, white dress, gloves and a Panama hat. Each girl in the dormitory had a chair and a table. Initially, the convent had no running water or heating except oil stoves. Eventually, the school installed bathrooms, which the borders shared.

Father Eugene Roulin died in a Leeds Nursing Home on 31st March 1939, aged seventy-eight. A few years earlier, he had an accident where he broke his leg. His age and failing health did not allow the broken bone to repair itself, and this was a big disappointment to the active father, who resigned himself to his faith and religion. Filey is proud of the heritage he has left behind.

Sadly, following the new comprehensive education system in the late 1960s, the convent school closed, as Filey had no other comparable school to merge. The nuns left Filey for their various apostolates elsewhere, and the building, purchased by Scarborough Urban District Council, became Filey's Town Hall. Today the building is the Evron Centre, and a plaque denotes a mark of respect for the nuns who selflessly made a lasting impact on its pupils and the people of Filey. The Evron centre now serves as a Community and Business centre, with meeting rooms, a lecture room, and Concert Hall.

A Filey Convent School 'Old Girl' reunion happens each year on the first weekend after Easter.

St John the Evangelist and the Iron Church

St John's credit Margaret Rounding

In the mid-19th century, religion and gospel studies were revived from all religious denominations. The Industrial Revolution gripped the country, and with the implantation of the railways, people moved around the country more freely. The demand for church services was especially apparent in the seaside towns, which increased throughout the summer. New churches were built throughout the country, and old ones were renovated and modernised. Filey was no exception, especially in summer when St Oswald's Church was full. Many of Filey's visitors stayed on the other side of town, making access to the parish church more difficult. Therefore, it was proposed to build a new Anglican church for the town.

Tin tabernacles or Galvanised Corrugated Iron Churches solved Filey's problem. This type of church could be constructed quickly and provide a temporary solution to the overcrowding whilst funds were raised to build a more permanent church building. In 1857, land for such a church was found on the east side of West Avenue, midway between Brooklands and Southdene. However, purchasing this structure was the subject of a London Court case.

In court documents, Miss Catherine Legard is described as 'A Lady of Fortune' and a relative of the Legard family of Ganton, who owned Filey's North Cliff Villa. Miss Legard had seen the structure in a catalogue whilst visiting an exhibition at the Crystal Palace of London. She had agreed with the manufacturer, Mr Hemming of Bow, to purchase the Iron Church at seven hundred and fifty pounds, which would be erected and delivered solely on Miss Legard's credit.

Iron Church era 1857 – West Avenue-Credit-Filey Town Council

However, other congregation members were not impressed with the idea of such a structure for their church and preferred to wait for a more permanent one. The Rev. Thomas Norfolk Jackson said of the purchase of the church, 'having foolishly (assumed) all risks of an Iron church, we are in an anomalous state.'

Subsequently, when the church was nearly completed and ready to be sent by railway to Filey, there were significant differences of opinion regarding the design and structure of the church. Hence, the church was not erected, and Mr Hemming found himself out of pocket and sued Miss Legard in the London Courts for breach of contract and damages.

In February 1857, at the Court of Common Pleas in London, in front of a special jury. After hearing evidence for the plaintiff, his Lordship suggested that Miss Legard asked the plaintiff to erect a church, and that is what he had done and that by not accepting the church, Miss Legard was in breach of contract. The jury agreed and found in favour of the plaintiff. Miss Legard assumed the responsibility, and the Iron Church was transported to Filey and erected as a temporary measure. Reverend Thomas Norfolk Jackson delivered a daily service at half-past ten and three o'clock.

In 1864, Admiral Robert Mitford of Hunmanby Hall was a parish patron. He donated land on West Avenue to build a new church. The curate Rev. Pettit and his friends raised fifteen hundred pounds towards the cost of the new church of St John the Evangelist, and parishioners raised the balance of seven hundred pounds. The church was built in a geometric architectural style, comprising a nave and chancel with transepts. A stained-glass window on the east side is dedicated to the memory of Admiral Mitford.

The church was consecrated in 1870 and licensed in 1874. It was altered in the 1970s and then converted to a smaller church, including a much-needed church hall.

Filey's Interesting Incumbents

The Reverend Evan Williams

Filey's parish church of St Oswald's has had many incumbents, but we remember two for their eccentricities in the early 19th century. The first one's peculiarities may explain the growing disillusionment with the town's institutionalist status quo of religion.

Between 1809 and 1833, Rev Evan Williams was a curate at St Oswald's. There was no vicarage, so he lived alone at 33 Church Street. The Reverend would not enter his house by the door. He also went in and out of the house by the windows. His further oddities were that he would let no women in the house. When the local dairyman delivered milk to the property, he had to do it via a pitcher that the Reverend would let down on a rope from an upstairs window. He would only spend one shilling's worth of fish for his food each week. Also, he would begin service at church, then say there was no sermon and go home, locking the church door behind him. Hopefully, he let the congregation out first.

An exciting story is told about him in 1823 when, at the bedside of one parishioner who lay dying, the unfortunate man asked that he may receive the last sacrament, and the conversation went:

Rev. 'Do you swear?'

Sick man 'No.'

Rev. 'Do you ever get drunk?'

Sick man 'No.'

Rev. 'Do you owe any money?'

Sick man 'No.'

Rev. 'Well, you are alright then! But you owe me money for your father's gravestone. I cannot give you the sacrament until you have paid it!'

The dying man settled the bill with the Reverend, received absolution, and died satisfied.

Rev. Williams was not happy with the way churchwardens were selected. Instead of them being the choice of one by the parishioners and one by the vicar. It had always been customary to be chosen by the parishioners. Reverend Williams challenged this tradition in court, but his lawsuit found favour with the established practice at the cost of ninety pounds to the church.

The Reverend Arthur Neville Cooper

Credit Stephen Eblet

Later in the 19th century, the Reverend Arthur Neville Cooper became the vicar of Filey. In 1905, he told his parishioners that he was the only incumbent in England who could not nominate a churchwarden. This right had been withdrawn from the vicar of Filey some years earlier when the churchwardens sold the lead from the church roof to buy food for starving parishioners.

Reverend Cooper earned the title 'The Walking Parson', as in 1886, he walked from London to Filey (200 miles.) A year later, he walked to Rome, some 743 miles. In the succeeding year, he repeatedly walked across Ireland. Then from Hamburg to Paris. He also walked extensively across Belgium, Spain and Venice. The Reverend Cooper walked at a pace of 30 miles per day, but on one occasion, between breakfast and supper, he covered 48 miles. Cooper said he carried no luggage except what he could fit into a rucksack when asked how he did this. He even tore up letters he received on his journey to ensure he had no excess weight. The Rev Cooper gained his passion for walking while working as a clerk in London, where he had to walk through all weathers four miles every morning, repeating the same journey on his journey home.

Before setting off on his journey, Reverend Cooper would study the language of the country he travelled to. He thought this to be essential in some of the small towns he visited. He wanted to converse with the locals.

S.14552.   REV   CANON A. N. COOPER VICAR OF FILEY.
(THE WALKING PARSON)

The Local Workhouse

Low Hall Hunmanby

Low Hall, on Sands Lane, Hunmanby, became the workhouse for the area in 1785. This workhouse had an average of 16 inmates and took in paupers from around the parish, including Filey, Flamborough, Burton Fleming, and many others.

The cost to convert the workhouse was expensive, costing two hundred pounds to make it fit its purpose. Eighty-seven pounds were collected from the poor rates. Squire Osbaldeston (Hunmanby Hall) provided twenty-four pounds and six shillings. A further sixty pounds was donated from the 'town stock'. Equipment purchased included sheets, baking dishes, coal, and food. Although the food at the workhouse was ample, it lacked variety and vitamin content. Although meat, potatoes and molasses were on the menu, there is no mention of green vegetables on any surviving workhouse diet sheets.

The poor hated the workhouse, and the government was terrified of encouraging lazy people, so they made sure that people feared it, and families knew it was the last resort and would do anything to keep out of it. The reason for ending up in the workhouse varied. People were too poor, old, or ill to support themselves, lacked work, had high unemployment or had no family willing to help them through poverty or illness. Unmarried pregnant women were often disowned by their families, and the workhouse became their only option. Interestingly, the master of the poorhouse in 1791 was Mr Thomas Dinnis, who fell on his luck when he was discharged from his duty and paid off. In August of that year, he went to Scarborough races and lost all his money on a horse. He was subsequently declared destitute and faced bankruptcy proceedings at York Assizes.

Here is a brief history of what happened to 'poor households' before abolishing the Poor Act in 1929, when the Poor Unions were abolished. The administration of poor relief was transferred to the counties and their boroughs.

From 1601, The Poor Law Act allowed local parishes to look after their poor. These poor people could live at home and claim assistance from the wealthier householders of the local parishes. As is much the same today, these upper and middle-class people were not impressed. They assumed that their money was being spent significantly on lazy people, who were avoiding work, as the cost of providing for these people was growing more expensive year. A fairer system was sought to prevent the current system from being abused by scroungers, and after years of upper-class complaints, the Poor Law was introduced in 1834.

Many old parishes formed poor law unions with this new Poor Law, which clubbed together to provide a workhouse for their community. Following the introduction of this act, poor people, who previously would have relied on a parish handout to survive and provide for their families, could no longer live at home. Instead, if people did not work hard, the whole family would be sent to the workhouse.

Over the years, there have been various legacies left to the poor. One of the earliest recorded was in August 1697, when a yeoman named Elisha Trott from Muston left an annuity to the poor of Filey of twenty shillings, which was payable out of a house and land he owned in Cayton named *The Rooks*. The will stipulated, 'If the property tenant withholds the payment, the overseers or churchwardens shall enter the house and remain there until the money is paid.'

This law did not account for tramps and vagrants, a police matter. Subsequently, tramps and vagrants were known as 'the houseless poor' and, if caught, would have to be set in the stocks for three days and three nights. They only received bread and water. If any 'vagabonds' were found begging, it would be customary to be stripped naked from the waist upwards and whipped until their bodies bled. A tramp or vagrant could be a shipwrecked seaman, a fortune teller, an Egyptian, a gipsy, or even a discharged prisoner. The worst type of vagrant, who was considered the scum of the earth, was an able-bodied person refusing to work for the current pay rate.

Hunmanby Workhouse closed in 1836 when Hunmanby joined the Bridlington Union, and a sizeable purpose-built workhouse for one hundred and fifty inmates was built in Marton Road Bridlington. After 1930, the poor law system ended, and the Bridlington workhouse was taken over by East Riding County Council and renamed Burlington House to provide accommodation for geriatric patients.

The Atlee Labour Government of 1945-1950 introduced the welfare state and finally abolished the workhouse system.

Old Filey

Ever since the Norman Conquest, the manorial rights of Filey have appertained to the Lords of Hunmanby. Walter de Gant succeeded his father, Gilbert de Gant. Walter founded Bridlington Priory. Filey Church had no incumbent, but the town was served by a stipendiary priest provided by Bridlington Priory. Six of the Gants in succession have held this Manor, some of whom have given lands in Ganton to Bridlington Priory. Most probably, the village of Ganton derives its name from this prominent family.

Ralph de Neville succeeded the Gants, who gave half a carucate of land to the same priory. His son (also named Ralph) donated 'to God, and the church and monks of Bridlington, the stone and stone quarry of Filey for building their monastery, and all their offices.'

Of some note, Filey was a fishing town as Bridlington Abbots, Whitby, and Grimsby quarrelled about the tithes. In 1122, the first prior had a dispute with the Abbot of Whitby, arranged by arbitration of the Dean and Chapter of York that they should pay tithes when Filey fishermen put into Whitby. When the fishermen of Whitby put into Filey, they should pay tithes at Filey. However, further disputes arose, for in 1190, Hugh, Abbot of Bridlington, complained to the Court of Rome of injustice done to him: when the pope, Celestine, commissioned the Abbot of Rievaulx and the Priors of Kirkham and Warter to examine the case. These justices decided that the Abbot of Whitby should never more molest the fishermen of Filey when they went into that port and obliged him to relinquish all claims to any tithe from them.

Changing Street Names and Demolished 'Yards and Rents'

The earliest detailed map of Filey dates to 1788 and is 'The Enclosure Map.' Filey comprised Town Street (now Queen Street) and Church Street at its right angles. The frontage of these streets was densely built up around both sides of Town Street and to the west of Church Street, which both had elongated 'yards or tenements running on the south side of Town Street and the west side of Church Street to 'Back Lanes' which are now Mitford Street and Scarborough Road.

This arrangement is typical of English settlements from the 12th century onwards, and before 1788, the structure of the main street and back lanes was little changed since medieval times. Following 'Enclosure', many of Filey's street names changed, with some roads or 'rents or yards' disappearing completely.

A substantial selection of land in Filey was advertised for sale in the Yorkshire Gazette in 1855, including 'Back Lane', which then became Mitford Street with new houses and shops.

AT FILEY,
In the East Riding of the County of York.

TO BE SOLD BY AUCTION, at the PACK-HORSE INN, in FILEY, in the East-Riding of the County of York, on FRIDAY, the 9th day of November next at TWO o'Clock in the Afternoon, (subject to such conditions as shall then be read,) Mr. ROBT ALLISON, Auctioneer, the whole of the Valuable PROPERTY, as follows, viz. :—

LOT 1.—All that Freehold DWELLING-HOUSE, situate in the Front Street in Filey aforesaid, with a Yard and Garden behind the same, now in the occupation of Mary Bulmer.

LOT 2.—A Freehold DWELLING-HOUSE, adjoining to the last-named Cottage on the East, with a Yard and Garden behind the same, now in the occupation of Grace Robinson.

LOT 3.—Three Freehold DWELLING-HOUSES, two of them in the Front Street, and one of them in the Back Lane, with a Yard behind, now in the occupation of William Cammish, Thomas Holmes, and John Cowling.

LOT 4.—A Freehold DWELLING-HOUSE, in the Back Lane, with a Yard behind, now in the occupation of John Chapman.

LOT 5.—A Freehold DWELLING-HOUSE and SHOP, in the Back Lane, with a Yard behind the same, now in the occupation of William Marshall.

LOT 6.—A Piece of Freehold GROUND adjoining the last-mentioned lot on the South, with several small Erections thereon, containing 108 square yards or thereabouts, now in the occupation of Messrs. Cammish, Cowling, Marshall, and Chapman.

LOT 7.—A Piece of Freehold LAND, principally used as a Garden, adjoining Lot 6 on the South, containing 284 square yards or thereabouts, at present in the occupation of William Marshall and John Chapman.

LOT 8.—Two DWELLING-HOUSES, in the Front Street, and Two behind, with a large Piece of GROUND behind the Dwelling-Houses, containing 1,444 square yards or thereabouts, at present in the occupation of Francis Clifford, Robert Wiseman, William Sayer, and Benjamin Grice. A Communication to this Lot from the Back Street will be reserved.

LOT 9.—A Piece of Freehold GROUND, admirably adapted for a Building Site, containing 669 square yards or thereabouts, situate behind the Pack-Horse Inn, and fronting the Back Street on the South, at present in the occupation of Mary Storey.

LOT 10.—A Piece of Freehold GROUND, adjoining the last-mentioned Lot on the East, containing 859 square yards, having the same frontage, and being similarly adapted to building purposes as Lot 9, also in the occupation of Mary Storey.

For further Particulars apply to the Auctioneer, at Bridlington; to Mr. Sheriton, Hunmanby, where a plan of the premises may be seen; or to

Messrs. BRUMELL,
Solicitors, Morpeth.

Yards

Off Murray Street, in between what is now Filey Bistro and The Three Tuns, was Cambridge Yard. In 1905, Captain Robert Groves, the head of Filey's Fire Brigade, is recorded as living at no 8. All the houses are now demolished. There were also five houses on the same street in Jennings Yard (where Smart's Stores are now).

There were many 'yards' off Queen Street, such as White's Yard, between houses 61-63. Then Richardson's Yard was between 75 and 77 Queen Street, comprising five houses occupied by fishermen and their families. Stockdale yard was between 81 Queen Street and Goodlad's Grocers (1905). Again, all the houses have since been demolished. Stockdale Yard housed fishermen with familiar surnames we still see today, such as Sayers, Jenkinson, Cammish, Scotter, Watkinson and Cowling. A fisherman kept a monkey in a cage in one of the fishermen's backyards.

At 41 Church Street stands Wenlock House, named after Lady Wenlock, a regular visitor and admirer of Filey. This house can be recognised by an anchor found in Filey Bay. In 1892, this was the home of the Suggitt family, who owned the coble Zillah named after Mrs Suggitt. The Suggitt's are the same family whose son Thomas met his demise in tragic circumstances after plunging to his death on Filey Brigg whilst looking for natural artefacts.

Between Wenlock House and number 39, and through a narrow passage, stood nine houses known as Wenlock Place. The 1851 census records sixty people living there. Private George William Skelton was born at no 5 Wenlock Place in 1893. He joined the Coldstream Guards and fought in the Great War but lost his life aged 23 and died from gunshot wounds to the chest and abdomen.

Changing Street Names

41-51 Mitford Street, previously Alma Terrace

Chapel Street, previously Brick Garth

27-41 West Avenue, formerly Clarence Terrace

3-21 Scarborough Road – East Parade

Between 7-8, The Crescent, previously Middle Street

Belle Vue Street, previously North Street

42-46 Belle Vue Street, formerly Prospect Place

89-103 West Avenue, previously Ravine Bank

Crescent Hill, previously Ravine Road

24-38 Rutland Street, previously Rutland Terrace

Reynolds Street, previously Skelton Lane

Between 14-15 The Crescent, South Street Station Road, formerly Summerville Road.

10-14 Station Road, previously Moore Lane & West End Terrace

38-54 West Avenue, formerly Westfield Terrace

West Road, originally Common Right Road

Filey's Ancient Market and Fair

On the site of where now stands the Forge Garage once stood Filey's courthouse. This area was aptly named Court-Garth, once the Court of Bridlington Priory, for the dispensing of justice and the transaction of business. In later years, around this area was the house of Filey vicarage, now Ebenezer Terrace.

The vicinity of the Court House was also the place of Filey's ancient market, initially held on a Sunday. However, on 22nd August 1240, King Henry 111 made a grant to William de Neville that the day of the market was changed to Friday. The reason given was that this market was damaging Gilbert de Gant's market at Hunmanby. However, this was not the end of this disagreement. In the autumn of 1242, Gilbert de Gant brought a case against William de Neville regarding the market at Filey, contending that William had broken this final concord.

On 29th May 1256, King Henry 111 granted the burgesses of Scarborough the right to plead in the king's court for the abolition of the Filey market and its fair. The markets of Sherbourne and Brompton are to be suppressed to benefit the burgeoning population of Scarborough.

The market cross was at the junction of Church Street, Scarborough Road, Mitford Street, Station Road (originally Moore Lane), and West Road (originally Common Right Lane). They led to Corn Mill, where the streets were widened to form a small marketplace, most likely dating from 1221.

Queen Street. The Hub of the Community.

Queen Street was the centre of the community. For many years, this bustling street housed the families of most of the village. Morning greetings from the street's many fishermen who made their way to their boats would be familiar. Fishing was an integral part of the town, and many of the fishermen's houses were defined by a glazed coble or drifter in their front door panel. Unfortunately, many of these have either been replaced or have disappeared.

Over the years, Queen Street has had a few different names. In the late 18th century, it was named Town Street as it was the main street in the town. From Cliff Top to Reynolds Street, it was Queen Street, and the rest was King Street. The street was buzzing with shops, craftsmen, fishermen, and rope makers.

In the mid-19th century, the newly established 'New Filey' residents were often born outside the town and did not have the same closeness or community as the 'old Filey' residents had. King/Queen Street was a major thoroughfare, with lots of shops supplying most of the community's needs, and there was no need for anyone to venture elsewhere, not even to 'New Filey'. The only people who had to cross Murray Street regularly were the girls and women working in the new hotels and boarding houses on the 'other' side of town.

Numbers 8-10 Queen Street is now the museum but was previously a farm cottage and a fisherman's cottage. The post office was initially at number 79, then moved to the corner of King Street and Reynolds Street before moving to Murray Street.

In 1895, Filey formed its own Urban District Council in purpose-built offices at 52 King/Queen Street. Its first elected chairman was Mr W Maley. In addition, they began a Highway, Improvement, Finance, and Fire Brigade Committee. A resolution was found that nineteen hundred pounds could be borrowed at an interest rate of 3.5% to be repaid over thirty years from the Wolverhampton Corporation, Sinking Food and Stock, to meet the cost of drainage for the new offices. To oversee the laying out of the foreshore. The council advertised in the local press for a clerk of works. Subsequently, they appointed Mr William Gofton and his grandfather at a salary of forty-five pounds per year. However, works on the seashore were unsatisfactory, and the Council refused to pay the contractors, resulting in litigation in the High Court.

Health was a significant consideration in the town, and Filey Urban District Council appointed a medical officer, Mr T Haworth, who presented his first report in January 1896. His findings for the quarter ending 31st December 1895 stated that there had been twenty-two births and twelve deaths, seven of which were over sixty, two between the ages of fifty/sixty and two infants under the age of two, and one premature birth. Deaths for the year totalled seventy-six, which was higher than the national average. Still, Mr Haworth said that twenty-seven of the deaths were children under twelve months and twenty-three over the age of sixty and that problems of pneumonia, influenza and bronchitis had attributed to the deaths in the very young and the very old. Mr Haworth also reported that the town was free from infectious diseases, remarking that the new drainage system had improved the sanitary conditions of the town, which now competed favourably with all other seaside resorts.

Many of the public houses on Queen/King Street remain. Such as The Foords and The Station, but a few have gone. The Pack Horse at 78 Queen Street was a thatched property whose last licensee was a lady called Elizabeth Kilby before the premises were demolished and The Crown Hotel erected in its place. The Britannia stood on the corner, now 65-71 Queen Street. The last landlord was Mr Edward Gutherless, who in 1882 faced charges for keeping his house open beyond permitted hours. The coastguard John Hilman and a labourer William Crow were also charged with 'drinking after time'. However, following a court appearance, all charges were dropped when both men confirmed they were friends of the landlord and no money had changed hands for the drinks. Shortly after, the premises were declared unfit for purpose and demolished.

Queen Street still keeps an affectionate remembrance for many people, although sadly long gone are the various shops, pubs, fishermen's cottages, rents and yards. However, many people recall the atmosphere of this once bustling, vigorous street which remains a vital part of the community.

Filey Builds a New Sea Wall

Old Sea Wall

Before the building of the sea wall in 1894, Filey's foreshore was divided into two parts. One part was protected by a wooden hulking, and the second was supported by damaged and corroding cliffs. Ferocious storms and mighty seas had battered these cliffs for years. A severe storm in 1864 dislodged hundreds of tonnes of earth, washing away part of the cliffs and dramatically affecting the town's staple trade. The fishing community was concerned that should there be another storm, the fishermen could not go to and from their landing, which was their only available access to their cobles and livelihoods.

Coble Landing Before the new Sea Wall.

Coastal erosion continues to be a severe problem. Filey's quest for a new sea wall began as early as 1874. The sea was making serious inroads into the cliffs, which unquestionably became a dominant consideration, as the land was disappearing at two yards a year. Urgent action was needed, or the sea would swallow up the houses on the foreshore. Plans for a harbour scheme had not come to fruition. Therefore, an ambitious project began protecting the foreshore and providing Filey with the most fashionable promenade.

Work on a new sea wall for the town started in 1892 when forty Filey residents (all men) formed a committee. The president was Mr Edwin Martin of Ravine Hall, who kindly donated one hundred pounds towards the expenses for the opening ceremony. His stipulation to this generous offer ensured that the poor people of Filey were not hassled for donations towards the scheme.

The building of the wall was not without its problems. Many of the town's ratepayers objected to the project's cost, and there were many other obstacles to overcome. Consent from the Admiralty was required, and they also had to agree to waive their rights to the foreshore. Interestingly, had the Filey local board did not propose the plan when they did, it would have been the Admiralty's responsibility to step in and protect the coastguard cottages.

The owners of the properties fronting the foreshore had to either contribute to the scheme's cost or grant concessions over their property. Difficulties had arisen when gaining consent from Miss Elizabeth Elders of Church Cliff Farm, one of Filey's biggest landowners. Eventually, an agreement was reached, and a provisional order was obtained, giving the committee the go-ahead.

The board advertised for plans to be drawn. Engineers Messrs.' Fairbank & Sons, Driffield & Westminster were appointed, with James Dickson of St. Albans contracting the building work. The building costs were estimated at twelve thousand pounds. The board arranged a loan for this amount from the Ecclesiastical Commissionaires. One stipulation was to repay the loan within ten years. (Because of unforeseen circumstances, the cost of the wall escalated to £15,000.) The Admiralty contributed three hundred pounds towards the scheme.

After discussion with the committee, Lord of the Manor, Colonel Mitford, of Hunmanby Hall made stone available from the Brigg at one farthing per tonne. In October 1893, work began, and two thousand tonnes of cement were delivered and spread across the beach to form a railway from the Brigg to allow the transportation of twenty thousand tonnes of stone and shingle.

The length of the sea wall from Ravine Slipway to Crescent Hill is seven hundred yards. The plans considered the depressed road surface in front of the Spa saloon, which was continually flooded in high water and eroded rapidly back then. A slipway was built parallel to the wall. A margin of grass of about ten yards was constructed, with seats and alcoves that provided aesthetic rest for the weary traveller.

In front of a large, lively crowd, the first twenty thousand concrete blocks were laid in April 1893 by Mrs Martin of Ravine Hall. The contractor's son, Mr James Dickson, handed Mrs Martin a silver trowel and ivory mallet inscribed: 'Presented to Mrs Edwin Martin, on her laying the first block of the Filey sea wall and promenade, 24th April 1893. Engineers Fairbank & Co; contractor James Dixon.'

Then, to a proud and excited crowd, Mrs Martin gave three taps of the mallet, and the block laid into place, and she declared in a distinct voice, 'I declare this block properly laid.' Reverend A.N. Cooper blessed the wall and those engaged in its building.

Laying the foundation stone

The trowel and mallet used by Mrs Martin remain in possession of Filey Town Council. Over two hundred men were employed in the construction. Besides having their missionary, they were also provided evening classes on reading and writing by local schoolteachers, Miss Pym and Miss Brown.

The contractors completed the building works on schedule. The wall opened in June 1894 to a rejoicing town in party mode. With their characteristic Yorkshire hospitality, the townsfolk decorated the town with coloured streamers and welcomed visitors from all over the country with signs saying: 'Welcome to Filey'.

Lord Herries, the Lord-Lieutenant of the East Riding, conducted the opening ceremony. For his services, the town presented him with an ornamental key. The wards formed an 'H' and bore suitable inscriptions. The key was surmounted with a coronet. Lord Herries then unlocked a temporary wooden barrier and declared the sea wall open to the public, followed by tremendous applause.

Without the determination and providence of this committee of people. Despite many obstacles and objections, they persevered and provided the town with a necessary defence barrier. Their fortuitous foresight concerning the design of the promenade added a new era to the town's popularity as a holiday resort. They were securing Filey's position as the jewel of the Yorkshire coast for many years to come.

Lord Herries opens the Sea Wall.

The Fishing Industry

An early picture of the Coble Landing

FFor centuries, the staple trade of Filey has predominately been fishing. Sadly, in October 2013, this all changed when the last coble, *Kathryn and Sarah,* owned by Julian Barker, left Filey, thus ending centuries of family tradition, hard work and industry. This coble was taken to Bridlington, refurbished and renamed *The Helena.*

This was a far cry from 1858, when Filey fishery was at its maximum strength when most of the town's inhabitants had some connection with fishing in their families.

Before the Industrial Revolution, fishing and selling wools were the nation's wealth and sustenance sources. As early as AD 211, there was a great abundance of fish along the northern shores of Britain; Dion

Cassius and Solinus, the latter of whom stated that the people of The Hebrides derived a principal part of their food from fishing, remarked on this. In 836, the Netherlanders visited the North-East coast to buy saltfish.

By the late 1500s, the Dutch fishing industry was solid, so much so that in 1603 Sir Walter Raleigh laid before the King a pamphlet urging the advantages of vigorous prosecution. He reasons that the most significant number of fish ever known in the world was on the Yorkshire Coast, yet the English people derived no benefit from it. They exported no herrings, yet the 'low' countries and other smaller states fished herring mainly along these coasts, with an annual income of seventeen hundred pounds. Before this, Hollanders and Flemings' custom before they felt on the Yorkshire Coast to 'crave leave' (seek permission) from the Governor of Scarborough Castle. In 1608, they paid tribute to King James for this privilege, and in 1635, they paid King Charles no less than thirty thousand pounds for permission to fish in the English seas. A colossal amount of money in those days.

As previously mentioned, 1857 was a successful year for Filey's fishermen, with a reported fleet of 64 inshore cobles, 17 herring cobles and 34 yawls. The coble was the most common in gardens and yards, with numbers spotted on coble landing and all over the town. Fishing follows a year-round pattern, whereby the yawls laid out in Scarborough over winter would be refitted out ready for the season, which begins in February to early June, to line-fish for cod, halibut, and haddock. Six men and three boys manned each Yawl. They carried two cobles and mainly fished off the Dogger Bank. Mid-week, the fish caught would be collected and put onto one Yawl, taking it to market at Hull, Scarborough or Filey, leaving a coble and three men to continue fishing the rest of the week. The gross proceeds were then divided into seven shares. One belonging to the boat, out of which expenses were paid, and the rest paid between the remaining men who provided the lines, bait, etc.

The coble was mainly used in winter and manned by three men who each took three lines – seven hundred yards long and carrying one hundred and forty hooks. They travelled as far as six miles to sea in winter between December and January. Filey fishermen took on the dangerous waves while the larger boats lay by. Filey cobles went out to fish at daybreak, not knowing when or if they would return. Twenty stones of fish were an excellent average catch for each coble, comprising haddock, codlings, and 'spring fish' (between a codling and a cod). The year 1857 was very successful, with a staggering twenty-seven thousand pounds (a substantial amount, £2234,620.00 in today's currency – 2022.)

The Fishing trade is hazardous and is weather-dependent, with the town benefitting from a 'Good Fishing Season' with most of the proceeds distributed around the town in wages, purchases and tradesmen. Other areas benefitted from this success, including the net manufacturers of Scotland. The rope and sailmaker of Hull, and the shareholders of The North-Eastern Railway, helped with the cost of the two thousand pounds to import herring around the country.

Filey Fishermen with their nets

Bonzo Filey's Pet Seal

While fishing on Filey Brigg in January 1927, local man Jack 'Bonzo' Jenkinson found a baby seal. The pup was in terrible condition and weighed only one stone. Mr Jenkinson rescued it, named it Bonzo, and the seal would perform tricks in time. Bonzo was put in a tank in Providence Place (Jenk Alley), then Coble Landing. The tank required a change of fresh water daily. Bonzo lived on a diet of fresh fish and was a constant attraction and source of amusement to visitors, including Princess Royal's two sons, when they holidayed in Filey.

Mr Jenkinson charged visitors a 'copper' to watch Bonzo do tricks and push his snout in and out of the water.

Twelve years later, Bonzo weight twenty stones and needed more and more water. In 1939, Mr Jenkinson's brother was looking after Bonzo when a bailiff from Filey Town Council called on him on a bicycle. The bailiff had court papers stating that Mr Jenkinson owed twenty pounds in unpaid water charges and demanded that 'he had come to take Bonzo.' Bearing in mind the size of the seal, it doesn't seem that the bailiff had thought about the logistics of how he would remove the seal, especially as the only transport the bailiff had was a bike.

Mr Jenkinson was devastated, and news of the seal's fate soon spread. Offers flooded in one from Golden Acre Park Leeds, who will take the seal. Mr Jenkinson was adamant that the seal should stay in Filey and hoped he could arrange it with the council. However, it transpired that Mr Jenkinson could also not afford the rent on the shed which housed Bonzo. Thus, Mr Jenkinson received a notice of twenty-eight days to vacate and find another house for the seal. Filey Town council was unrepentant and got an order from the court to allow them to put the seal up for auction. At the last minute, a solution was found when Mr Smith of Church Cliff Farm allowed Mr Jenkinson to keep the seal on land he owned on the Foreshore, and the seal continued to entertain visitors for some time. Bonzo died in 1940 of natural causes.

Flither Girls

Bait is vital for fishing, and the fishermen dug large quantities of worms from the beach for this purpose. The curl of the sand recognises the location of worms they leave behind on the surface. Together with 'war fish' or 'Razorfish' (as they are commonly known), these are also dug up. These small fish are identified by a little cup-like depression in the sand with a hole in the centre. These spring tides are taken at low water when the fish is seen sticking up an inch or two out of their holes. In addition, bait named 'lamperns' would be imported from York, London and Nottingham.

This fish is excellent bait, and one piece sufficed four hooks, each boat taking two hundred a week. In 1867, these cost nine shillings per hundred, and the weekly consumption was six thousand from early February to Good Friday.

The most exciting and lamentable method of procuring bait was the rough and hazardous labour of the fishermen's wives, widows and daughters. Who were relentless in their endeavours and would go out in all weathers to find bait by skeining the mussels (whereby a live mussel is taken from its shell and scooped out). This is hard and tedious work, and from December to June, these strong, hardy women and girls would ransack the rocks for flithers (limpets). Unfortunately, the supply of flithers on the Brigg was deficient because of constant demand. Therefore, the women had to travel to nearby Gristhorpe.

To shorten the distance and reach some parts of these rocks otherwise deemed unapproachable, these resilient bait gatherers descended the cliffs a few yards beyond Newbiggin-Wyke Wyke at a place called 'Chimney Hole'. They did this using a rope fastened around their waists and secured by a small, unsafe-looking stake placed at the top of the cliff – usually in a hole in the cliff. The women would descend about 40 feet, hanging for dear life onto the rope, with their feet firmly planted against the cliff side whilst they hurriedly searched for bait.

Chimney Hole

In 1863, the Volunteer's steamship was wrecked on 'the horseshoe rock' close to the cliffs. This is where the ladies sought their bait. Men descended onto the wreckage and brought loads of broken timber and supplies rummaged from the wreck on their backs. The flither girls, once they had filled their three baskets, which they called 'mawns', would come up the same dangerous way.

Photograph credit Ian Nisbet

These committed women were genuinely incredible and meticulous. When the Gristhorpe rocks were devoured of all bait, and to satisfy the needs of the fishermen, the women would, week after week, leave Filey by train (they walked before the convenience of the railway) to Scarborough. They would then walk nine to ten miles to Claughton and Hayburn Wyke. They would leave home on Monday-Tuesday and return on Friday/Saturday. During this time, they would take up lodgings and pay for food, all for the reward of the sale of three baskets of bait.

It was a novel sight to witness the girl's return. A carriage was attached to the evening train specifically for them, and a separate truck for their bait baskets. Friends would wait at the train station to see the girl's return when the catch would be distributed between the prospected purchasers. The exhausted yet excited girls were always pleased to be home safe and well. Filey train station was alive with the high-pitched chatter of the Filey dialect, which was often misunderstood and considered by visitors as 'Moosel gathers chit-chat.'

Fishing Disasters

The orphaned children of Robin Jenkinson (insert), who lost his life on The Research

The immense loss of lives and property on our seas to shipwrecks has been tragic and costly. In such a small community, it was not unusual for families to lose many members of the same family in one event.

On 25th November 1925, most families were excitedly preparing for Christmas when this tragedy happened. A great sorrow was given over grief-stricken Filey where, following a storm at sea, the entire crew of a steam drifter, The Research, were lost.

One family faced a hazardous future as the father, his two sons, and two of his son's in-laws perished, leaving five widows and eight fatherless children behind them. As he was known locally, John Robert Jenkinson or Jack Sled (1862-1925), was the head of the family and skipper of *The Research*. A fearless man who had saved many lives without recognition. His two sons, Robin and George, were fishermen and sailed with him that fateful day. Robin had six children, and George had two. His two sons-in-law were William Cammish and George Crimlisk.

Jack Sled's family was dogged by tragedy. His half-brother, known as 'Dick Sled', Richard Cammish Jenkinson (1846-1918), lost his son and two of his grandsons, who were blown up on the *Emulator* in 1919 by a German Mine. Another of Jack Sled's sons, James Henry Newby Jenkinson (18921911), was lost in 1911 off Ravenscar, aged 19. When it capsized, he had been working with two other men on the herring coble Swanland Hall. Jack Sled was a strong swimmer and tried to save the three men by getting them all onto the upturned boat, but as he got one on, another would not let go of the keel and fell back into the sea. Sadly, Dick Sled's son James drowned with another man named George Scales. Sadly, James was about to become a father, and the shock of his drowning sent his wife, Mary Ellen Jenkinson, into labour. His daughter was born shortly after.

The drifter *The Research,* owned by Messrs. Melrose of North Shields, was an old vessel in poor condition. In hindsight, it is easy to assume that the drifter was not entirely seaworthy. It is known that *The Research* shot her lines and had been fishing off Flamborough Head when the storm struck. Newspaper reports state that the last Filey men to see the crew of *The Research* alive were 'Denk' Major and Mark and Rueben Scotter. Who was on a steam drifter heading for the shore in the face of deteriorating weather? As they passed within 60 yards of *The Research,* Rueben called, 'it's time you were gettin' in, Jack. Run for Brid.' The crew waved to 'Denk,' and he waved back. Within an hour, the drifter and the crew were lost. The drifter hit its bottom on 'Smethwick Sands', a large shoal in Bridlington Bay. The sea would have easily swamped her if she were stuck fast. She might have been safe if she had stayed offshore in the deeper water.

Remains of the wreckage were discovered two days later, off Hornsea. The wreckage comprised a fisherman's oilskin, a gaff (a kind of boat hook) and a piece of wood that bore marks Y and Figure 42 which shows the registration mark of *The Research,* which was Y.H.421. Two fish boxes were washed ashore with the inscription S.U.S.T Co Ltd, the company's name from Scarborough, managing the vessel.

The family was close, living a few doors from each other in Clifford's Yard and 41 Mitford Street. To add to their suffering, they had not only lost their loved ones but also their breadwinners and sole providers. Being share-fishermen, the bereaved widows were not entitled to a widow's pension under the then Widow and Pension Act of 1925 and relied on well-wishers' donations to survive. A fund was quickly started and advertised in the press. Public sympathy was high, and funds soon accumulated. Scarborough Football Club, Bridlington Yacht club, and The Leeds Mercury were some of the first to offer generous subscriptions. A memorial to *The Research* and all the lives lost is in St Oswald's parish church.

Sadly, in February 1939, Jack Sled's widow Fanny Elizabeth Jenkinson, then aged seventy-six, was told of more tragic news. Her grandson had fallen overboard off a motor keel in Whitby and drowned. The sea had already robbed her of her husband, three sons, and two sons-in-law. She had recently been seriously ill, and relatives and friends feared that this latest shock could kill her.

Her grandson, Tom Scotter, aged 33, lived with his wife and child in Scarborough. He had been a fisherman for twenty years.

Mrs Jenkinson only had one son left, and after *The Research* disaster, she pleaded with him to leave the sea; he did and took a job as a roadman with the council. She has said, 'I know what it means, for a man must work, and women must weep. My life seems haunted by tragedy, but if I had my time again. I would still marry a fisherman.' Her epitaph at the family grave at St Oswald's churchyard reads: 'She suffered much but murmured not.'

Filey Lifeboat

In 1823, local historian Mr Thomas Hinderwell started an appeal for Filey to have its lifeboat and Lifeboat station. Mr Hinderwell was persistent and bombarded many newspapers in York and Hull with his and many people's concerns over the recent storms and the continual loss of life at sea. Following his appeal, contributions came in, and in 1823, Filey had its first lifeboat. Unfortunately, this first lifeboat was unnamed and housed on the foreshore near Cargate Hill. This lifeboat was manned by volunteers and run as a local undertaking unit. Unlike today, the lifeboat relies on sail and oar for their motive power, whereas the lifeboat station uses an inshore vessel in emergencies close to the shoreline.

In 1853, the RNLI took over the running of the lifeboat. The various lifeboats have saved many lives throughout the years. Thanks to the bravery and dedication of the coxswain and the lifeboat crew. In 1863, Filey received its first lifeboat to carry a name; it was Hollon, named in honour of a great benefactor, R.W. Hollon – a former Lord Mayor of York. This lifeboat was replaced twenty-one years later by Hollon II and followed twenty-three years later by Hollon III. These three vessels saved the lives of one hundred and sixty-nine people during their seventy-four years in service.

Old Lifeboat Station credit Emma Guy

Hollon II

The naming of Hollon III 1907

In 1940, Filey received its first motorised lifeboat, *The Cuttle*, named after another benefactor, Mrs Rosemary Cuttle of Rotherham. *The Cuttle* saved twenty-eight lives during its thirteen years of service. *The Cuttle* was replaced in 1953 by *The Isa and Penryn Milstead*. This boat served Filey until 1968, followed by the boat *Robert and Dorothy Hardcastle*.

The Cuttle 1953 (*Photo: John Holroyd*)

The Isa and Penryn Milstead

The Robert & Dorothy Hardcastle

To be the Coxswain of a lifeboat is a great honour, and Filey is lucky to have had such competent Coxswains over the years. Barry Robson served the town very well, following in the footsteps of Graham Taylor, who, together with the highly trained and brave young people, worked as volunteers to protect the lives of distressed people at sea. Coxswains have included Crompton Wyvill, Richard Cammish, Thomas Cappleman, etc.

There have been many tales of lifeboat rescues over the years. In 1839, the crew of the *Medusa* from Whitby were rescued after a heavy storm. Captain Ruddock was at the helm, followed by many volunteers who quickly doffed their jackets, watches etc., and bravely rescued six of the seven men. The seventh, a young eighteen-year-old gentleman, insisted on securing some of his clothing and missed his opportunity to jump into the lifeboat. Despite many brave attempts to save him, the young man lost his life.

Filey is indebted to the Coxswain, the crew, and the volunteers who continue to support this valuable and much-needed service.

In April 2021, after 220 years, Filey lost its all-weather lifeboat and was replaced by an in-shore boat. A very emotional day for the town. A spokesman for Filey RNLI said, 'times change, casualties change, you need to be faster in response to incidents, and that's certainly what the Atlantic 85 will do, between 40-45 miles per hour. So, it can be all over quickly.' A sad day indeed.

George Dingle Scales Lifeboat Coxswain 1894-1907

Filey Railway

Credit Stephen Eblet

Filey Railway station opened on 5th October 1846. The York and Midland Railway Company operated the first train, which left York station at 11.30 in the morning, heading for its first journey to the coast. This train had five carriages filled with dignitaries, including the chairman of the railway company Mr George Hudson and The Lord and Lady Mayor of York.

The train was decorated with flags and banners and reached Seamer station an hour later, then onto its destination: the new Filey station and an eagerly awaiting crowd. Architect George Townsend Andrews, who worked on many railway designs for the eminent Mr Hudson, had designed the station. The station was a single-storey red brick structure with a slate roof and sandstone dressings, with a seven-bay main entrance projected from the station. The train shed roof was a standard design for Andrew's, using a wrought iron truss structure supporting a wood and slate roof.

Arriving at Filey, the townsfolk were out in force. A public holiday was declared, and four hundred children lined the street with placards and flags. Mr Bentley had provided barrels of ale from his brewery and two sides of beef for the locals. Inside the station, the walls were adorned with silk banners saying: 'Success to Hudson and The York & Midland Railway.' Another said: 'Prosperity to the town and trade of Filey.' Afterwards, there was a procession through the town. Mr Bentley Esq of Ravine Hall laid on elegant carriages to transport the dignitaries to his mansion for an afternoon celebration luncheon.

George Hudson was a financier and politician who inherited a large sum of money (£30,000) from a distant relative at age twenty-seven. A relative he barely knew. He invested most of his money into the railways. Thus, he controlled a significant part of this new form of transport, earning the title 'The Railway King.' Hudson's financial dealings were dubious, often paying shareholders out of capital rather than profits. In 1849, railway officials enquired into his financial dealings, revealing a series of irregularities. Hudson suffered severe financial pressure and lost his Conservative seat in Sunderland. Facing bankruptcy, he went to live abroad to avoid being arrested for debt, only returning to England when the law for imprisonment for debt was abolished. Hudson named none of his co-conspirators, who, despite reaping the rewards in good times, turned their back on him when the going got tough.

Initially, Filey railway station included a goods yard, a coal depot and gas works. The fishing industry benefited from the implantation of the railways to transport fish to areas not previously thought possible. The railway opened Filey up as a holiday destination, with people able to travel there and back by train at their convenience.

Goods traffic ceased to Filey in 1964, and the station was made a Grade II Listed Building in 1988. Recently, improvements have been made to the interior and exterior of the building. The station is used each day by passengers travelling all over the country.

Education

Prior to the 1870 Education Act, schooling in rural areas was predominantly a matter of chance, cost and the availability of someone willing to offer educational instruction, usually a self-educated spinster from the local neighbourhood.

During the early 19th century, education in Filey was deficient, especially for the poor and the working classes. The Wesleyan Methodists, who had their schoolroom on West Avenue (now Dixons), provided day schooling. The Wesleyan school was immediately adjoining the chapel, comprising two large schoolrooms, one on the ground floor and one above each, accommodating one hundred infants.

Filey's Mechanics Institute was at 6 Clarence Place, with a circulating library open to all visitors. In the winter, classes were held for adult members of society who wanted to learn to read and write. Many fishermen took advantage of this, as they'd never learned. Educated public members devoted their time and services for free and included the notorious Dr Edward William Pritchard (former local doctor and later a convicted murderer) for a brief time.

Filey had a generous share of privately run schools. One of the most popular was Clarence House. A private, purposely built girls' school run by the formidable Miss McCullum. The school offered a 'High-Class Education' specialising in French and German. The school closed in 1930 after 70 years, when it briefly became a hotel, then a youth hostel. At one time, there was a talk that the building would be demolished, but luckily that was not the case, and it is now converted into privately owned flats.

On 28th September 1928, in connection with The Wesleyan Association, London, Hunmanby Hall, the old residence of Humphrey Osbaldeston Esq, opened its doors as a private secondary school for girls. The first headmistress was Miss Frances Hargreaves, B.A, who had a degree in history. She was a minister's daughter who had been assistant head at Kent College for girls.' Miss Hargreaves assured parents of a non-Wesleyan denomination that arrangements were in place for the girls to attend the local parish church. Many alterations were made to the building, including new bedrooms, sanitary arrangements, tennis courts, and other playing areas. The old laundry was converted to provide five new classrooms, and the dining hall was extended to accommodate two hundred pupils. Hunmanby Hall continued as a successful school until 1991. It is now privately owned flats.

The Crescent, again, offered private schools. There was Brookville School for girls run by Miss Holmes, and at no 6 Rutland Terrace, next door at number 4 was Miss Gardiner's Boarding Academy.

Breaking up from School for the summer. Boarding school on The Crescent. Author's Collection.

The largest private boy's school was Southcliffe Primrose Valley, established in 1901 as a preparatory school for boys aged 7-14. The headmaster was Rev. A.H. Gaskell, and under his headship, tuition was given for entry to public school. This tuition included music, languages, riding, golf and swimming (the school had an indoor swimming bath – a luxury for any school). After the school closed, the premises became a hotel, then a pub (Churchills) and later part of the Haven holiday chain. Unfortunately, it is now closed and in a dilapidated state of repair.

There was a smaller boy's school at no 2, Clarence Terrace. Offering only a few spaces for boarders. In 1891, the school advertised, 'This school is especially adapted for delicate or backward boys' who require healthy bracing air with home comforts and individual training.'

For Filey children, many of whom came from working-class or poorer families, education was provided by Filey's church school, built-in 1839 on Scarborough Road. The school did not have a good reputation and was inadequate for the needs of the pupils. The school was enlarged in 1846, vastly improving the premises and facilities. However, the school had severe problems.

In 1879, the school's head was Rev. Basil K Woodd, the then Vicar of Filey, and the school was open to all religious denominations. In December of the same year, a case was brought against the school owners before Magistrate Colonel Prickett at Bridlington Police Court. The claimant was Mr Frederick Buxton, the local Sanitary Inspector for Filey. The owners, Rev. Woodd, Mr William Beswick (Gristhorpe,) James Haworth, Robert Smith, Robert Cammish, and George Watson, all from Filey, were ordered to appear. The charges were 'That in or upon The Scarborough Road, in the parish of Filey in the district under public health Act 1875 of the Filey Local Board, and of which premises you are the owners, the following nuisance exists: Namely:

Defective drainage

Want of a winter closet

A supply of water

Ventilation

Damp walls

And a specific contagious disease and the said nuisance is caused by you, the owners!

The chief defendant was Rev. Woodd, who had been given a chance to rectify the complaints without escalating matters further. Still, he ignored this warning and did not facilitate any repairs. Therefore, the sanitary board received no further option than to seek justice in court.

The circumstances were that in October 1879, an epidemic of Scarlatina broke out in Filey. The medical officer for health and the inspector of nuisances concluded the epidemic did not arise in the other church-run schools, attributing it to the defective sanitary arrangements of this state church school. Rev. Woodd received formal notice to remedy the dire state of the drains, but unfortunately, he ignored it.

The claimant described the state of the school's closets, which he stated were built under the school's walls and directly abutting the latter. He said the contents had to be seen to be believed and overflowed into the playground and percolated the school walls.

Another complaint was that there was no water connected to the urinal. The complainant deposed that 'there was no water laid on the school, the ventilation filled with dirty rags, and the walls of the school walls were all unhealthy'.

The court case was dismissed on a technicality (the Inspector failed to get the whole board's backing before issuing proceedings). However, following this report, the school was demolished, and a new national school building was built on the same land.

Filey Infants/Junior School Scarborough Road Circa 1990

A new Junior school opened on Mitford Street in February 1900. Captain Mitford generously donated the land, and the cost to build it was two thousand five hundred pounds, which was raised entirely by donations.

The school was designed by a local man, Mr Robson and constructed using only local tradesmen and labour. The school accommodated two hundred and fifty pupils with a large hall serving as a Parish Room. Sledmere Court is where the school used to be.

Infant's School Mitford Street

In 1946, as the town grew, the two streams were combined with infants, who started their school days at the Mitford Street school—later going on to the Junior School on West Road. A new school was built on Scarborough Road, then finally on to the Secondary School at West Road to accommodate new pupils. The town was again expanding, so a new school was built on Muston Road, becoming the secondary school (now Ebor Academy).

The Mitford Street school closed in the early 1960s. Infants were moved to the Scarborough Road School and juniors to West Road. In 1988, a new infant school opened on Padbury Avenue and Scarborough Road school was abandoned. (It was demolished in 1999). Private houses were built on the land, and the street was named Church View in memory of the school.

Filey's Prominent Buildings

Filey has many splendid buildings. Some helped shape Filey's history but have long since been demolished or remodelled as hotels, guest houses, or luxury holiday flats. Gone are the days when noblemen or women built marine Villa residences for their love of the bracing sea air.

Cliff House

The Glasshouse and Charlottes Cliff House were one of the first houses built to develop 'New Filey' circa 1824-1855. For a brief time, the house enjoyed unrivalled sea views across the 'German Ocean' until the completion of the Crescent in the late 1850s. The original owner of Cliff House was Francis Smith and his wife, Eleanor. The Smiths had the honour of sheltering the creator of *Jane Eyre*, Miss Charlotte Bronte, who was a regular visitor to Filey.

Charlotte Bronte loved the sea, which came close only to her love of the moors. Charlotte had been ill for some time and thought a trip to Filey and a change of air would do her good. She stayed at Cliff House in June 1852 and wrote to her father from there on 2nd June, in which she beautifully and characteristically expresses a direct reference to Filey. Here is a short extract from that letter.

'On the whole, I get on very well here, but I have not bathed yet as I am told it is much too cold and too early in the season. The sea is very grand. Yesterday it was a somewhat unusually high tide, and I stood on the cliffs watching the tumbling in of great tawny turbid waves that made the whole shore white with foam and filled the air with sand hollower and deeper than thunder.

'When the tide is out, the sands are wide, long and smooth, and very pleasant to walk on. When the tides are in, not a vestige of sand remains.'

She also wrote to her lifelong friend Ellen Nussey on 6th June 1852 again from Cliff House:

'I am in our old lodgings at Mrs Smith's, not in the same rooms, but in less expensive apartments. They seemed glad to see me, remembered you and me very well, and seemingly, with a great goodwill. The daughter who used to wait on us is just married. Filey seems to me to be much altered; more lodging houses, some of them very handsome, have been built, and the sea has all its old grandeur.'

After Charlotte Bronte died in 1855, Ellen Nussey devoted her life to maintaining the memory of her friend, who she had first met at Roe Head High School near Dewsbury in 1831. Over the years, they wrote hundreds of letters to each other, which fortunately have eventually made their way to The Bronte Parsonage Museum in Haworth.

Interestingly, the novel *Jane Eyre* was rejected five times by various publishers. Unperturbed, in 1847, Charlotte sent the manuscript to Smith, Elder & Co (London) following advice from her friends William Wordsworth and poet laureate Robert Southey that 'Novel writing was not the pastime of a lady.' She sent the manuscript under the pen name of Mr Currer Bell. The publishers took the risk, and *Jane Eyre* became the fiction masterpiece we know today.

Miss Bronte is not the only famous writer to have stayed at Cliff House. The writer J. E. Buckrose was a regular visitor to the house in the early 1920s. The novelist, Mrs Annie Edith Foster Jameson, stayed there with her husband, Mr R. Falconer Jameson. Cliff House was owned by Mr Frank Wordsworth Jameson and his wife Ethel Maud Marion Jameson, the brother of the writer's husband, who had moved to Filey from Hull. J. E. Buckrose wrote over forty books, including *'Love in a little Town* and *The Gossip Shop.'* She used Yorkshire as the setting in all her novels.

In June 1921, a tragedy happened to the Jameson family. At about 2 p.m., Mrs Ethel Jameson went for a walk to collect wildflowers from the cliff at the top of the Brigg. Robin Jenkinson (who would later lose his life on *The Research*) and Cyril Gannon were at the bottom of the cliffs collecting wood when they heard a thud. Initially, they assumed that a part of the cliff face had eroded and slipped. On closer inspection, they found the lifeless body of a woman sitting upright, wedged between two large boulders. The body had rebounded from a two-hundred feet fall as Mrs Edith Jameson fell over the edge. The inquest recorded a verdict of accidental death. The coroner praised the police officer PC Beckett for his bravery and for making a tricky descent of the cliff by ropes to recover Mrs Jameson's body.

Cliff House has been extensively remodelled and is now known as The Glasshouse, a bar and restaurant. Fortunately, the grapevine remains.

*

Church Cliff House and Farm (Parish Field's House)

Church Cliff House. Author's Collection.

Agriculture has been a mainstay of Filey's economy for centuries. Our ancestors have farmed Filey's hills and pastures since Neolithic times. Yorkshire was predominately an agricultural county well up to the nineteenth century. Farming is necessary to feed the population, and many people, including children, were employed in the industry. The work is brutal, with very little rest bite and small rewards, working all hours and constantly fearing adverse weather, which could ruin the year's crop. Farming was not just a job. It was a lifestyle often involving the entire family.

The Industrial Revolution affected rural communities, with people migrating to towns and cities with the promise of industrial work and improved living conditions. Before this, agricultural work was the country's biggest source of employment. The work was hard, and the master expected their men to work seven days a week. Most of the work was manual, and innovative machinery became available, improving productivity and decreasing the need for additional farm hands.

Horses were necessary on the farm and integral to Filey's community. They pulled the many agricultural implements that tiled the soil. They hauled produce from the field to farm and farm to market. The farmers would supply horses to the fishermen to help pull their boats when required. The blacksmith smithy on Mitford Street would have been busy with many horses to shoe.

Horses. Church Cliff Farm, circa 1880. Author's Collection.

Farming in Filey continues today but on a much smaller scale. In the nineteenth century (some remain today), Filey and the surrounding villages had many farms. I name a few, Moor Farm, Howe Farm, Hunmanby, Muston Grange Farm, Newbiggin Filey, Manor Farm Filey, Low Fields Farm, and Craik (Crayke) Farm Muston. No 10 Queen Street (where the Museum stands now) was also a farm run by dairy farmers, the Gibson family, who still farm in the area.

In 1909, Mr & Mrs Saville from Craik Farm was Filey's unluckiest couple. In 1909, they lost their eldest son to a motor accident. He ran into the road, and a car ran him over. Six months later, on Christmas Eve, a large car collided with their horse and cart while travelling home from Scarborough, swinging the carriage around into the car's wheels. The couple's second son narrowly escaped death. The car failed to stop.

In chapter twenty-five (Enclosure), we read that farming in Filey was based on traditional agriculture and the open field system. The local economy depended on three large arable fields and a common pasture surrounding the village.

Until the Enclosure Act of 1791, Filey relied on this farming system, whereby Rye, Wheat, Oats, or Barley and then Fallow ensured that each field would be used each year differently. In Filey, each strip was owned or tenanted by villagers. In chapter twenty-five, we saw Great Field, Church Field, and Little Field.

Over time, and despite the advantages and the social benefits this system brought to communal village life, this system became increasingly uneconomic. Combining the strips of land and enclosing larger fields with walls and hedges was necessary.

Manor Farm, on Mitford Street next to the Star Pub, was owned and operated by the Wilson family. Following the death of her husband, son and daughter, Mrs Wilson ran the farm herself. In 1896, Mrs Wilson faced a heavy fine in the Bridlington Court for failing to inform the authorities that one of her cows had died from Anthrax. She had reported it to Mr Leppington of Hunmanby Cow Club, who had instructed a vet to bury the dead animal at Hunmanby. Mrs Wilson was fined forty shillings plus costs and Leppington five pounds. Fortunately, this was an isolated case.

Church Cliff Farm, Church Cliff House and the adjacent Parish Fields are an essential part of Filey's heritage and, as a farm, were the most extensive estate in Filey.

In the 1840s, Richard Lowish owned the farm. However, he found himself in financial difficulty, and despite selling all his rams comprising sixteen shearlings and nineteen of different ages, he still could not make ends meet. In 1843, he assigned all his possessions to his creditors and gave up farming at Church Cliff Farm.

Mr Elisha Elders and his family were the next occupants. Elisha Elders was born in Egton on 26th March 1799. He married Jane and had four children: Mary, Ann, Newman and Jane. Jane died in infancy. Elders was a good farmer, and the family was well respected within the Filey community.

Interestingly, the two Elders' daughters married brothers. Mary, the eldest, married Mr AW North of Hull on Xmas Eve at St Oswald's Church Filey, while Ann, the second daughter, married her sister's husband's brother, Mr TH North, in July 1857.

The Elders owned various properties in the Filey area, including farms at Gristhorpe with a farmhouse and outbuildings with one-hundred and forty acres, of which thirty were 'Old Sward'. (A lawn or meadow) They also owned Crake House Farm at Muston with fifty-four acres. Both farms adjoined each other. Both these farms were offered for sale in 1855 by public auction at

In 1859, Elisha Elders appeared before Bridlington Courthouse for non-payment of Highway rates. Mr Richardson appeared on behalf of the surveyors. Mr Donner (Scarborough) acted for Mr Elders. In Mr Elders defence, he objected to paying his rates because the surveyors paid certain sums over to the nuisance removal committee to make drains in Filey town. Mr Elders did not see why he should have contributed to this expense.

Mr Richardson stated the surveyors had to pay over to the local committee under the Nuisance Act. Such sums for the required works and the highway rates could not be challenged, withheld, or objected to by ratepayers.

The magistrates agreed with the claimant and ordered Mr Elders to pay his rates and the associated court costs.

Elisha Elders. Author's Collection.

A year before he died, Mr Elders was at Seamer Fair, where he lost his valuable gold pocket watch and its chain and appendages. He remembered looking at the watch. He thought that he had put it back in his pocket. Luckily for him, the watch was found in the street and handed in by a sincere cattle dealer from Bishop Burton. On hearing of his watch's safe return. He was showing his gratitude. The elderly farmer handed the cattle dealer a rich reward.

Author's Collection

Elisha died in 1865, aged sixty-six. Here is a picture of Mrs Elders mourning at the gate of Church Cliff House with her two daughters.

Following her husband's death, Mrs Elders ran the farm for a short time. The Elders also held extensive property in Back Lane Filey, which they sold in 1861.

In 1891, Miss Mary Elders continued to live at the farm. She voiced her objection to the new sea wall. However, this objection was soon overcome.

In 1925, Wharton Elders sold his beloved 1924 five-seater Chevrolet tourer motor car for one hundred and ten pounds as he left Filey and moved to South Africa to continue farming. He married Christine Dreyer, and three children were born in South Africa, with Agar as a middle name. He died in 1975 in Bloemfontein, South Africa.

Mrs Elders with her daughters. Author's Collection.

The Smith Family

Robert Smith lived with his family at his father's farm, Howe Farm Hunmanby. He was forty-seven when he married Zillah Agar Suggitt, twenty-five years his junior. Zillah was the eldest daughter of Thomas Suggitt of Wenlock House, Church Street.

The couple moved to Church Cliff Farm soon after their marriage. The couple had nine children, Robert William, Frank, Charles, Tom, Zillah Agar, Mary Harriett, Charles, Sarah Edith and Wharton.

Robert died in 1890, aged seventy-three. His sons Tom and Charles took over the running of the farm.

Charles Smith Weight-Training Church Cliff Farm

Author's Collection.

1898 Filey Shooting Church Cliff Farm.

The Stackyard Church Cliff Farm. Author's Collection.

A terrible case came before Filey Police Court in 1898. In September that year, twenty-one-year-old Edwin Johnson from Muston, a chargehand working at Church Cliff Farm, Filey, was accused of attempting to murder his work colleagues.

Johnson was a shy and reliable person. He was attending to his duties together with Mathew Milner, George Coultas and the brother of the farm's owner, Charles Smith, who was working on a haystack in the corner of the farmyard. The usual waggoner was away, so Johnson asked his master who would take the wagon that day. Smith responded Milner was the most likely man for the job. Johnson did not expect this reply, as he was the foreman and would have expected the duty to go to him. In a huff, Johnson stormed off and went to Scarborough, where he bought himself a pistol and some cartridges.

The following day, he returned to the stackyard on the farm and recited a religious text loudly. Realising that Johnson was quite unhinged, Charles Smith tried to calm Johnson down. Johnson told Smith that he would not hurt him. He asked to see the master Tom Smith who he held a grudge from the previous day. Suddenly, Johnson fired a shot into the air and demanded to know who was doing the stacking. He was told it was Matthew Milner, enraged Johnson replied, 'that he was a devil to take a man's job away from him!' Milner cautiously climbed down the stack when Johnson pointed the loaded revolver at her ten yards away and fired.

 Fortunately, Johnson was a poor shot, and the bullet narrowly missed his intended victim. He tried another shot and again missed. In a very excited state, Johnson's noise of the firing altered other workmen who rushed at Johnson while others ran for the Police.

When Johnson saw the Police coming, he reloaded the gun, placed the muzzle to his temple, and fired. He fell instantly to the ground. The doctor came and admitted Johnson to the hospital in critical condition.

The bullet lodged in Johnson's brain was removed, but he lost an eye, and the prognosis was that he would eventually be completely blind in time. Johnson was remanded in jail when he was fit enough and taken to trial for attempted murder. At the trial, the judge took all the circumstances into account mercifully. He fined Johnson ten pounds and bound him over to keep the peace for one year.

Fortunately, Johnson did not go blind. He went into Bridlington Hospital for an operation to remove the bullet lodged in his brain. Fortunately, his sight was saved. He later moved away from Filey and continued working on a farm. He died in Scarborough in 1968.

Zillah Agar Suggitt Smith was aged ninety-five, Filey's eldest woman. She died at Church Cliff Farm in April 1937.

In 1944, Church Cliff Farm and 320,439 acres of land were auctioned at the Three Tuns Hotel Filey. On 3rd September 1944.

One year later, the farm was purchased for twenty-four thousand pounds by a new company called Church Cliff Farming Company Limited, with nine thousand in one-pound shares. The directors were Mr & Mrs Taylor of Beechwood Driffield and Mr & Mrs Megginson of Grey Gables, Driffield.

Mr Taylor confirmed he had bought the land for speculation, which he later sold for development. (See Chapter on the sale of the Brigg) The farmhouse itself remains one of Filey's most prestigious buildings.

Ravine Hall

Credit Crimlisk Fisher Archive

Henry Bentley Esq, a brewer from the West Riding, built Ravine Villa in the late 1830s. The house was extravagant, with outbuildings, stabling, and an icehouse. The Bentleys bought the land to build the Marine Villa from John Wilkes Unett. The Villa was surrounded by two and a half acres of land with extensive views of the sea and the cliffs, together with a private walk and carriage road to the sands named Bentley's Gill.

The Bentley family-owned property in Yorkshire for hundreds of years. One ancestor was Dr Bentley, a celebrated master at Trinity College Cambridge, born in Oulton in the sixteenth century.

Henry married his first cousin, Maria Stocks. Maria was the third and youngest daughter of Michael Stocks, JP of Upper Shibden Hall, Halifax.

This once-great house was only one of the Stocks family's many residences. Michael Stocks rebuilt the Hall and renamed it Catherine House. Michael

Stocks was heavily involved with coal mining and brewing. Stocks was asked to be Halifax's first mayor, but he turned the role down.

Henry and Maria had three sons. Timothy, the eldest, was born in May 1831, Henry Junior in December 1832, and Frederick in 1837. There were two daughters, Eleanor, born in 1829 and her sister Mary the following year. Initially, they lived in the brewery building, but then they moved into the newly refurbished Eshald House in the early 1840s.

The Bentleys were a generous and popular couple. In 1858, when the railway came to Filey, Mr & Mrs Bentley provided a sumptuous tea party in their house's gardens and offered the locals free drinks and food, a much-appreciated gesture. The couple was also very prominent at St Oswald's Church. Mrs Bentley donated an organ there following a fire at the church.

Henry Bentley died in 1856, aged 45. His death certificate revealed he had jaundice for nine years and dropsy for six months. Both ailments are associated with liver disease. Mrs Bentley died six years later, aged 49.

Ravine Villa was advertised for sale in 1856. However, for some unknown reason, the sale was withdrawn. The house was then let on a year-to-year basis, including all the furniture.

Credit Crimlisk Fisher Archive

The Martin Family

Edwin Martin, a West Riding industrialist, and his wife Mary Elizabeth bought the Villa in 1889. The couple married in 1875 when Edwin was twenty-five and Mary Elizabeth was eighteen.

Mary Elizabeth's father, Henry Liddell, died suddenly when Mary Elizabeth was only ten years old, and her mother, Catherine, took over the family's boot and manufacturing company. Edwin took charge of his family's woollen factory. However, he wasn't at the helm for long, as he handed the business over to his younger brother, John William, in 1891.

The couple had six children, although the youngest daughter, Dorothy, died in infancy. The children were Edwin McGrath b 1877, Agnes b 1878, Margery b 1883, Francis Duke b 1884, and the last child, Dorothy, who was born and died in 1891.

Mrs Martin must have had a significant impact on the inhabitants of Filey, as she was the one who laid the foundation stone for the new sea wall in 1893. The Martins renamed Bentley's Gill Martin's Ravine, which is how we know it today.

The Martin's moved to Åfjord, Norway, in the late 1890s. After living there for a few years, the authorities allowed them to build a house they named Elvemo – Martin's Farm. Mr Martin settled in his newly adopted country, but Mrs Martin longed to return to their home in Filey. It seems Mrs Martin got her wish as the property in Norway was advertised for rent back in the UK. Mr John de Grey, who later became the 7th Lord of Walsingham from Norfolk, rented the Norway property from 1907-1910.

The 1891 census records the Martins living at Derwent Villa East Ayton with one son and one daughter. However, by 1911, the Martin's were back residing at Ravine Hall with five servants.

Mr & Mrs Martin at their home in Norway 1898.

Credit Geir Berdahl

The Martin's son Francis Duke Martin, born in Filey and educated at Uppingham School, Rutland, moved to Australia and enlisted in the 29th Battalion, 3rd Reinforcement Unit, where he achieved the rank of Sergeant. Unfortunately, Francis was killed in action in Belgium in September 1915.

In 1917, at the London Bankruptcy Court, Mr Martin's eldest son Mr Edwin McGrath Martin, living at Ravine Villa Filey, a solicitor previously carrying on business at Bloomsbury London, was declared bankrupt. Mr Martin had earlier written to the court to advise that he could not afford the travelling expenses to attend the meeting from Filey to London. It came to light that Mr Martin had lost three thousand five hundred pounds on the stock market, and he now had debts of eight hundred pounds and assets of twenty-five pounds. There was quite a stigma attached to bankruptcy, so this must have been unpleasant for Mr Martin. In contrast, in the same year, a nephew of the Martin's was knighted for supplying large quantities of uniform cloth to the British, French and Russian Governments.

Credit The Crimlisk Fisher Archive

Edwin Martin died in Filey in 1921. Mary Elizabeth Martin died in March 1929. She was aged seventy-two and had been ill for some time.

The contents of the Villa, including various paintings and antique furniture, were offered for sale in a public auction. In the same year, it was announced in the press (Skegness News) that negotiations were progressing concerning Filey town Council purchasing the Ravine estate from the family executors. The estate also included two fields in the parish of Muston and the house and grounds, which adjoin the golf links, lying between the sea and West Avenue. The council conceded that if the council should acquire such a desirable estate, which would lead to the town's future development and allow the council to launch into new enterprise for the benefit of Filey throughout the summer months.

At the monthly council meeting on 30th July 1929, the clerk reported that an Inspector of the Ministry of Health had held a public inquiry regarding the council's application to borrow sixteen thousand five hundred pounds to purchase the Ravine Estate.

The council's application for a loan was successful. In January 1930, one account passed for payment was sixteen thousand five hundred pounds for the purchase of the Ravine Estate paid to the executors of Mrs Martin.

The problem was, what did the council intend to do with surplus lands? Councillors agreed that the two fields formerly in the occupation of the Highways Department would be let on a yearly tenancy to Mrs Burr at a rental of thirty-six pounds per annum. Regarding the land adjoining West Avenue in the occupation of Mr J Gibson, the council agreed to impose conditions on any future tenancy that a condition is inserted in the agreement, limiting its use to agricultural purposes.

However, it seems the council was unsure of what to do with Ravine Hall, and between 1930-1938, the property was let as a private hotel/Guest House.

The following proprietors were the Wilson/Vaux family, who ran the Hall as a guest house, which could not have been easy in such turbulent times. In 1936, the local paper announced that well-known Filey/Bridlington architect Mr Fred Vaux had married Miss Doris Wilson, the daughter of Mr & Mrs George H Wilson of Ravine Hall, the couple married at St Oswald's, Filey. Miss Wilson was known within the Filey golfing community.

Credit The Crimlisk Fisher Archive

The hotel/guest house continued until 1939, when the war ended this enterprise. By 1940, the council had requisitioned the Villa.

There was talk of extending the building and adding a Floral Hall on the grounds. Tenders were invited to erect a large greenhouse, but this project was abandoned again because of the second world war. In 1946, the Villa opened as a council-run café which operated at a loss. The council then again let the property as a private enterprise as a café between 1947 and 1950. In 1954, it was used briefly as a boy's club. Between 1955-1960 it was occupied by a leather factory, which operated from the top floor. After this venture, the Villa stood empty.

In 1970, after considering the results of a public inquiry, the Ministry of Housing & Local Government gave Filey Council the go-ahead to demolish the Hall described as 'Filey's most distinguished piece of architecture. There was talk that East Riding County Council said it was considering placing a preservation order on the Hall. Thus, Filey Town Council demolished the building the year previously in 1969. They were concerned about the preservation order's cost, as no grants were available. Besides, the property was in a dilapidated state of repair with dry rot.

Filey councillors were concerned about the actual cost of demolition and considered what other purpose the Hall could have. Councillor Stevenson said the council had devised a plan incorporating an indoor swimming pool. Members also stated that the area could become another 'Sewerby Hall' if preserved. Councillor Don Mason told the council that it could be turned into luxury holiday flats and let them out at ten pounds a week. The councillors could not agree on the Villa's future use, but they all decided that the Villa was now an eyesore and a blot on the beauty of the town.

The demolition was stalled for one month while the commission for Historical Monuments completed either a record of the building or decided it did not want to record it. The once lavish marine residence was finally demolished in late 1971.

The grounds are now Glen Gardens, a pleasure area with a boating lake, a children's playground, and a café.

Filey Baths and Spa Company

Ackworth House

Spa Saloon 1872

During the 18th and 19th centuries, the fashion for spa towns was expanding across the country, and Filey was no exception. The new buildings on The Crescent, Filey, were receiving a much larger number of visitors than in previous years and rapidly gained a reputation as one of the most fashionable watering places on the Yorkshire coast.

Filey's hierarchy was concerned that because of a lack of spa facilities in the town, visitors travelled to the neighbouring towns of Scarborough or Bridlington, each of which had its own spa facilities. In 1861, it complied with visitors' wishes and offered these additional facilities. Subsequently, a company was formed under the 'Joint Stock Companies Ltd Liability Acts' named *'The Filey Public Baths and Saloon'*. The company's Directors were John Wilkes Unett Esq, Chairman, The Rev. T. N. Jackson, George Brown Esq, Mr Elisha Elders, Mr William Mosey, Mr Pattison, and Mr Robert Cammish. Two-thirds of the company's shares had been sold, but the rest were offered for public sale in The Leeds Mercury in 1861.

Building land was secured on The Undercliff (so-called as it was under the cliff) on Filey's seafront, and the property came equipped with hot and cold water, showers, and vapour baths. Together with a saloon, reading room, and a suitable dwelling for a manager, the premises were expected to be open in July 1861. In addition, bathing machines belonging to the premises would be available for hire. The cost of the building and all equipment was eight thousand pounds. However, this company's success was short-lived as the chairman Mr Unett announced on the 19th of June 1874 that the company w be voluntarily wound up.

An early picture of The Spa

Photograph courtesy of Joanne Cammish

In 1867, the York Herald advertised the property (not the business) for sale by public auction as 'Valuable freehold property. The advert stated, 'all the valuable and spacious building comprising: a large saloon, reading and reception rooms, six bathrooms, six lodging rooms, kitchen cellars and offices. The advert stressed that the property occupied an unrivalled situation in the centre of Filey Bay. If desired and subjected to the wishes of the overriding spa company, the property could be converted into one or more excellent marine residences. Immediate possession was offered. Mr Robert Cammish (one director of the Filey Public Baths and Saloon Company) bought the property. Before advertising for a new tenant, Mr Cammish ran the business for ten years. However, he still owned the freehold, and various tenants came and went over the years.

In 1880, a Mr Job Charles Chapman and his new wife Ellen (Ibbetson) were the new tenants. Ellen was originally from Ackworth and wanted to open the premises as a lodging house. Ellen renamed the premises in honour of her hometown as 'Ackworth Guest House'.

However, not everything was plain sailing for the newlyweds. In 1890, their landlord Robert Cammish instructed builders to undertake extensive decorations and rebuilding works, including changing the windows from the original gothic-shaped arches to the more 'modern' square rectangular windows, which we still see today. However, there was a dispute with the builder Mr Ruddock, who sued Mr Cammish in Scarborough County Court for twenty-three shillings and ten pence. The plaintiff argued he was employed to complete extensive decorations and alterations to the property. While most of the contract had been paid, this additional amount was still outstanding. The verdict was for the plaintiff, together with associated costs.

Over the years, many applications had been submitted to the Bridlington Petty Sessions for a liqueur license for the premises, arguing that the overspill of visitors from the highly popular Royal Crescent Hotel necessitated an additional license for the Ackworth, but the application was continuously refused.

In 1896, a newly formed company named The Hudson Hotel Company aggressively sought to buy a portfolio of hotels on the Yorkshire Coast.

Mr James Varley, who ran The Royal Crescent Hotel for over two decades, was one of the first to sell his premises for a considerable sum. The Royal Crescent Hotel, Ackworth Guest House, The Ravenscar, Robin Hood's Bay, The Crown, The Royal and The Queens Hotel in Scarborough were all acquired.

During the Second World War, many properties were commandeered by the armed forces, and subsequently, Ackworth Guest House became occupied by The Free French Army. This deployed regiment had a strong presence in the town, and its soldiers liked nothing better than to drink and dance with the locals on a Saturday night.

In 1947, Hudson Hotels leased Ackworth Guest House to CHA Countrywide Holiday's Association, and Ackworth House Hotel became the Association's first family centre. Still, despite this, the centre was for adults only, with separate male and female dormitories. No intoxicating liquor was allowed. Prayers took place each morning—Sunday services and grace were heard before meals. The host and hostess organised the evening get-togethers. These activities were an essential part of the CHA philosophy, with guests invited to sing, recite or discuss some topic of popular interest. The CHA's communal ideal was further emphasised through the insistence that domestic helpers at the centres were treated as equals and encouraged to join in leisure activities.

Hudson Hotels wound up its company in 1956. The Royal Crescent Hotel and Ackworth House were sold to the private sector. The Royal Crescent Hotel became privately owned flats. In 1982, Ackworth House became a well-respected and privately owned nursing home, and it remained until 2015, when the business was no longer viable. The property was sold to the private sector.

Ackworth Hotel

Photograph courtesy Joanne Cammish

North Cliff Villa

North Cliff Villa circa 1895

In 1830, there were only two houses in what is now known as 'New Filey'. The first was Mr & Mrs Smith's red brick residence known as Cliff House (now The Glass House, Bronte Vinery and Charlotte's Cafe), the farthest house in a southerly direction for many years. The second was William Voase's 'North Cliff Villa' villa, which he had built facing the sea. William was the son of John and Francis Voase, listed in the directory of Hull 1823 as a wine and spirit merchant and shipowner. The Voase later became the owners of Anlaby Hall. William Voase died in

1845, and Sir Thomas Digby Legard of Ganton Hall bought the villa and enlarged it to twice its original size, making it his occasional residence. Following Sir Thomas's death, the property passed to Sir Charles Legard, the 11th Baronet. Sir Charles sold the Villa in 1861 to Richard H Foord, the Rector of Foxholes and a Justice of the Peace.

In 1875, John and Margaret Gibson bought the property. John Gibson had previously spent fifteen years as The Pack Horse Inn (Queen Street, Filey) licensee, and he applied to the Brewster session in York for a liqueur licence for North Cliff Villa. He produced a photograph of the premises and numerously signed testimonials to support his request. The Licensed Victuallers Association in Filey opposed the application. Subsequently, the judge refused the licence citing that in Filey, there were already a third more licensed houses in proportion to the population than in Scarborough or Bridlington.

John Gibson died shortly afterwards, but his wife and children continued to run North Cliff as a lodging house until the late 1880s.

Filey 1860: Old North Cliff is visible at the far top of this picture

In 1890, a spinster named Miss Elinor Clarke bought North Cliff, ordered the immediate demolition of the villa, and commissioned the well-known architect Walter. H. Brierley to design a new substantial building. The villa, completed in 1892, is as it stands today.

Miss Clarke died on 4th January 1905, aged 63. In her will, she left the sum of £157,939 (equivalent today (2017) to £17,338,528.42), a considerable amount of money which led to speculation about the origins of Miss Clarke's fortune. Previous records recorded that Miss Clarke was a descendant of Scotland's wealthy Clark cotton family. She wasn't. She was no relation to this family (different surname spelling). Elinor's origins were closer to home.

Elinor Clarke was born in Chorlton on Medlock, Manchester, on the 18th of September 1842. Her parents were Robert Dennison Clarke and Jane Clarke (nee Skelton). Elinor's father, Robert, had his own paper-staining business in central Manchester with his partner, John Mush. Her mother, Jane, was a farmer's daughter from Wrelton.

Paper stainers were in most large towns. By the mid-nineteenth century, Britain was the world leader in the industrial production of wallpaper in terms of design and technology. Manchester arguably was the heart of this industry, and Mush & Clarke were trade leaders. Their premises were at 73 George Street, Central Manchester, a well-respected firm and much in demand. Before the mid-1700s, only the wealthy had to wallpaper from China, France or perhaps London. The paper stainer block-printed the paper by hand on relatively short lengths of paper. A register pin was set in each corner of the wooden block (which they carved themselves) to help locate the second and subsequent strikes accurately, and in this way, a repeat pattern was achieved. The paper might then be overprinted in a second or third colour in just the same way. They typically hung the paper for customers as well. A good provincial paper stainer would offer London and even French papers and his own. Until 1836, each sheet was taxed, and paper stainers also had to purchase a licence. Paper stainers were eventually driven out of business as demand grew for rotary-printed paper in long rolls, printed from engraved metal plates, as we know it today.

Seen below is a token advertising coin the company produced. (1844) To this day, tokens bearing Mush & Clarke are sometimes found around Manchester and surrounding areas and are occasionally offered for sale on online auctioning sites.

Robert and Jane married on 8th July 1837 at Collegiate Church Manchester (now Manchester Cathedral). The couple had four children, but unfortunately, a daughter, Mary, died in infancy. The surviving children were Robert Dennison (Jr), Eliza and Elinor. Initially, the family lived at 18 Robert Street, Chorlton, on Medlock, in a house they rented from a local landowner named Mr Tysick.

Robert and Jane had been married seven years when Robert contracted consumption. The disease was rampant in Victorian England, mainly because of poor water supplies, bad living conditions, and no preventative vaccines to stop the spread of the disease. Consumption or tuberculosis – so-called as it 'consumed' the whole body, with the patient's weight dropping drastically as the disease progressed.

Reports claimed that fresh air was the only cure for this dreadful disease. Therefore, Robert was sent to Scarborough to convalesce with Jane's uncle (Skelton boat-builders, Sandside, Scarborough). Regrettably, it was too late; Robert was beyond recovery. He died aged thirty-seven in Scarborough on 27th March 1844.

Robert did not leave a will, but he left a significant amount of money, ten thousand pounds. The Prerogative Court of York dealt with his estate. The Prerogative Court of York had jurisdiction over Cheshire, Cumberland, Durham, Lancashire and others. This court had the authority to grant probate or administration where the diocesan courts could not entertain the case. The deceased had died possessed of goods above a set value in two or more dioceses. Unfortunately, not long after, Jane caught the same disease and died soon after.

Following their mother's death, Elinor, her brother and her sister were baptised at St Saviour's Church, Manchester, on 6th August 1847. Before her death, Jane had planned that her children should be brought up and educated in the care of two spinster sisters, Elizabeth and Anne Alderson. The sisters were clergyman's daughters; their father was Rev. William Alderson, the Rector of Everingham. The sisters' brother William was a prison chaplain at Wakefield Prison. William was married to the poet and hymnist Eliza Sibbald Alderson nee Dykes, who wrote many hymns, including Lord of Glory, who has brought us together with and now, beloved Lord, Thy soul resigning. Eliza was also the sister of John Bacchus Dykes, the famous composer who wrote over three hundred hymns, including Holy, Holy, Holy Lord God Almighty.

Initially, the children lived with the sisters at Strawberry Cottage Matlock, recorded on the 1851 census as 'orphans and scholars at home.' Ten years later, the sisters and Eliza Clarke (Elinor's sister) lived at Wakefield Prison; Elinor taught at a private school in Lytham St Anne's.

Jane's brother John Skelton was also influential in the upbringing of his nieces and nephews and kept a 'fatherly' eye over them. John married Miss Ellen Brown in 1844. Ellen's father, Thomas Brown, was a wealthy landowner from Greenheys Chorlton-cum-Medlock. John and Ellen had a house built in Timperley named Pickering Lodge. This house, a rich and substantial residence with immaculate gardens, spanned 50 acres of land on Moss Lane and included cottages, then called Grove cottages. Unfortunately, not long after the couple moved in, tragedy struck the family again as Ellen contracted cholera and died shortly after.

Pickering Lodge circa 1915

The Alderson sisters moved to Filey in 1862 when Elizabeth and Anne purchased 1 Rutland Terrace. Architect Mr Elsworth had previously owned the property. In 1871, the census chronicled the sisters living there 'in the interest of monies.' The house's other occupants were their niece Caroline, nephew William, and the sisters' younger brother Richard, a surgeon. While Elinor was still teaching in Lytham, Robert and Eliza were busy with their lives in London and Croydon.

The Alderson sisters were excellent teachers, and with their direction, the children received a good standard of education. Robert Denison Clarke Jr studied law at Gonville & Caius College Cambridge, where he graduated with a bachelor's degree in Law in 1861, followed by a Master of Arts three years later. He was called to the bar in 1865 (Middle Temple), and Eliza got engaged to one of her brother's friends, barrister William Fox-Hawes. They married at St Oswald's Church, Filey, on the 1st of November 1866. They then moved to Croydon and later had five children. Unfortunately, Eliza died on 3rd April 1881, aged only 43. Her husband William remarried in 1884 and had another daughter, Caroline Fox-Hawes.

John Skelton (Jr) inherited warehouses in New High Street, Central Manchester, from his uncle George Wood and property known as The Polygon (Ardwick). In 1844, John Skelton agreed to let the High Street properties to John Rylands, Manchester's first multi-millionaire. The businessmen decided that Mr Rylands could join the properties and let them on a long lease. Until 2021 Debenhams occupied the inherited property in Chorlton (Chorlton Row) from his father-in-law Thomas Brown which he rented out. John's father died in 1860, leaving him on the farm in Wrelton. The cottages attached to the farm were again rented out, and the farmhouse became a pub named *The Bean Sheaf.*

John continued to invest in property. In Scarborough, he bought and developed *The Pavilion Square,* on which, in 1870, the *Pavilion Hotel* was built (later owned by the Laughton family). In 1860, he also sold part of his land in Timperley to the Timperley and Altrincham Railway Company to build a link line between Stockport and Warrington; his name is still preserved at the junction *Skelton Junction* (Timperley and). John lived at Pickering Lodge until 1873. He met and married Miss Elizabeth Lavinia Theobald, the daughter of the Rev. Thomas Theobald, the Rector of Nunnery and Private Chaplain to Lord Palmerston. The wedding took place at Christchurch, Clifton, Bristol, but then the couple moved to London, where they bought two properties, 36 Eaton Square and a rambling house in Forest Hill Park, Clewer (Windsor).

John made a will, leaving most of his possessions and property to his wife. However, Elizabeth died three years before him. Therefore, the will was amended, with the bulk of his estate going to his next of kin, his nephew Robert Dennison Clarke. Elinor, his niece, was bequeathed £5,000. His deceased niece's family (Fox Hawes) were left with the rents from the Polygon properties in Manchester, which were divided between them. John was also very charitable and bequeathed a sum of one thousand pounds, the income to be distributed at Christmas for the benefit of the poor at Wrelton and Cropton. John Skelton died on 1st June 1886.

Now a wealthy man and a considerable property owner, Robert Dennison Clarke (Jr) sold Pavilion Square, Scarborough and 36 Eaton Square, London, and moved into the house at Forest Hill Park in Clewer. Robert had a housekeeper called Emily King, who had a son named John Skelton Clarke King. What relation the child was to either Robert or John Skelton is unclear. However, in his will, Robert provided for these people for the rest of their lives. Trainee solicitor John Skelton Clarke King was killed in action in 1916, aged twenty-eight. Robert bequeathed the property he had inherited from his uncle and his estate to his only remaining relative, his sister, Elinor. Three years later, Robert died. He was fifty years old. The estate now reverted to Robert's next of kin, his sister, Elinor Clarke.

Elinor, now a woman of substance, sold many inherited properties, including Forest Hill Park, Clewer (which backed onto Windsor Castle). In his will, John Skelton bequeathed a freehold plot of land containing two acres, one rood twenty-six perches, and two cottages in Timperley (Formerly Pickering Lodge Estate). At the time of Robert Dennison Clarke Jr's death, this property was let to Mr Keymer at an annual rent of forty-five pounds. Mr Keymer was a Manchester merchant and farmer. In October 1893, Elinor Clarke sold the land and cottages to Sidney Keymer, who continued to let them out until he died in 1919. Around this time, Elinor also sold the houses in Wrelton.

Elinor, together with John Shaw, a well-to-do colliery owner of Darrington Hall, Darrington, was involved with the restoration of Welburn Hall in Kirkbymoorside, which had once belonged to the Squire Shepperd of Douthwaite Dale. The property had been empty for over one hundred years and required extensive renovation. Elinor spent twenty-five thousand pounds on the restoration, probably more than the house was worth. Elinor sold the property to Mr Shaw, who completed the renovations, adding a new kitchen wing, servant's hall, stables, and a gatehouse.

Exactly what Elinor's interest in this renovation is in writing (2017) is unclear. However, it may have been political, as Elinor was a staunch conservative, as was Mr Shaw. Possibly, Elinor was a member of the Primrose League, an organisation created by Lord Randolph Churchill (father of Sir Winston), whose membership welcomed women. Subsequently, many women joined in their droves. These members provided the party with a vast army of volunteers from constituencies nationwide. Elinor was most likely one of them.

John Shaw provoked notoriety in 1893 when he was defeated in the Pontefract election and brought a court case against his liberal opponent, alleging bribery of the electorate. (He was unsuccessful)

The Rose Garden North Cliff

North Cliff remains an imposing building with rambling gardens that extend to the seafront. Initially, there was a large greenhouse located where Belvedere Villa once was. (This house was demolished to accommodate this structure and to extend the gardens) Local rumours (not substantiated) say that Elinor wanted to marry Canon Arthur Cooper, the 'walking parson' of Filey and that she built North Cliff and its greenhouse to impress him. Elinor's 'devotion' to the Canon was unsuccessful even if this rumour was confirmed as the Reverend married the much younger Maude Nicholson in 1891.

The house has a separate cottage occupied by her driver, George Gofton and his family. At the back of the house was a piece of land that the locals named Clarke's Asphalt, where Elinor allowed the local fishermen to dry and mend their nets. There was also a separate 'meeting room', which Elinor donated as a community meeting room, primarily used by the boy scouts.

Fishermen mending nets at Clarke's Asphalt circa 1900

Elizabeth Alderson died at North Cliff, age 95 (her sister Anne had died five years earlier). She had been a mentor, friend, substitute mother, and educator to Elinor and her family.

Elinor Clarke died on 4th January 1905; she was 63 years old. She had suffered from gout for many years. Her obituary says, 'Elinor was a generous friend to the poor and the Church of England and true to the Conservative cause in Filey.' Before this, she had provided new choir stalls for Filey parish church. Miss Clarke was also one of the largest private donors of shirts and clothing to the troops during the war. The Yeomanry guard named a Maxim gun in her honour. At Elinor's funeral, Canon Cooper was physically shaking and visibly upset as he conducted the service.

Elinor left the bulk of her estate to her niece and namesake, Elinor Fox Hawes and the rest of her sister's children. However, she left a legacy to her driver, George Gofton and her other companion, Annie Swann and a small amount to her cook.

George Gofton, chauffeur to Elinor Clarke
Credit Joanne Cammish

North Cliff, the coach house and stables were advertised for sale in March 1905 and auctioned at the Foords Hotel. There was only one bid of five thousand pounds made by Mr William Barber of Scarborough. Subsequently, the sale was withdrawn.

The National Union of printers, bookbinders, and paper workers bought North Cliff in 1925, becoming a Convalescent home for its members.

North Cliff was a Convalescent Home.

In later years, North Cliff was divided into three separate privately owned apartments. However, in recent years, another intelligent private lady bought the flats, and they are again undergoing redevelopment and re-conversion to one large, elegant house.

Interestingly, Pickering Lodge, the house John Skelton had built-in in 1850 and later owned by George Hardy of Hardy's Crown Brewery (Cheadle Hulme), became the annexe to the Auxiliary Military Hospital at Heyesleigh, the home of Dr Lois Savatard. The Red Cross ran Heyesleigh Hospital. In 1914, this hospital had 15 beds. The number of beds was increased to thirty-six with the annexe at Pickering Lodge.

The then-owner, Sam Hardy, lent the property to accommodate casualties from the 1st World War. A marquee was erected at the hospital and, later, an additional hut at Pickering Lodge, bringing the number of beds to 98. Volunteers and donations helped to fund the hospital. One scheme was an egg collection organised by the local Church Lads Brigade, whereby the lads collected over six thousand eggs from local farmers and householders. Another scheme was arranged by local schoolchildren who collected horse chestnuts to be used as a substitute for grain in an industrial process. All the chestnuts were collected in baskets and then addressed to 'The Director of Propellant Supplies, Ministry of Munitions!'

Sadly, Pickering Lodge was sold for housing in 1920, and the council bought the house. Unfortunately, the house had become infested with dry rot. The cottages were demolished on 11 September 1941, after which the land became the public space known as Moss Park Gardens.

So, what happened next? Elinor Clarke left the bulk of her estate to her niece and namesake, Elinor Fox-Hawes, her sister Eliza's daughter. Elinor Fox-Hawes lived in Bournemouth until she died in 1956. Monies were bequeathed to Terence Fox-Hawes, a schoolmaster from Bournemouth. Terence died in 1991, leaving an estate valued at £49,564 3sd 11d. (101,666.72) Calculated in 2017. Elinor's other niece Caroline Fox-Hawes also a benefactor in Elinor's will, married a Belgium man named Raoul Robichon, who sadly died young at 43. Following her husband's death, Caroline lived at 30A Hanover Square, Middlesex, but died in June 1926 in Paris.

Elinor's housekeeper and companion, Annie Amelia Swann, inherited two hundred pounds a year for life from Elinor's will. Annie moved from Filey to St John's Wood, London, where records locate her as living off 'private means.' Elinor's faithful chauffeur George Gofton continued to live in Filey with his wife and family.

In his will, John Skelton's stipulated that the Fox-Hawes children should benefit from the 'chief rents' from the Polygon properties. However, in 1899, the children were subjected to theft. The accused was the solicitor, who was looking after their interests. The family accepted an offer of four thousand three hundred pounds to sell the 'rents' to Mr Wilkinson. A deposit of four hundred pounds was to be paid on the agreement and the balance on completion. Mr Wilkinson duly paid the deposit as agreed, but the solicitor Mr Robert Wooldenden used this money for private purposes. The solicitor had severe financial troubles and had filed for bankruptcy a week before, pocketing the deposit. Subsequently, the solicitor was jailed.

Elinor Clarke credit Ian Elsom

Elinor is buried in St Oswald's churchyard close to the ravine. In 1907 a stained-glass window was donated to the church by her nieces Caroline Robichon (nee Fox-Hawes) and Elinor Fox-Hawes in honour of their aunt. A fitting memorial to a memorable and often mysterious woman.

Elinor Clarke Window, St. Oswald's Church.

Filey's Public Houses

Throughout the years, locals and visitors have enjoyed a tipple in many of the town's licensed premises. In the mid to late 19th century, Queen Street was the hub of the community and the place to be. Local fishermen, tradespeople and their families used the various pubs as meeting places to chat and sample the local ales. At the start of the season, an influx of visitors wanting to get away from the grime and industrialisation of the city joined Filey's regular pubgoers. As they do today, the visitors came to take in the sea air, relax and mingle with the locals. Also, like today's visitors, they were a much-welcomed sight for a publican after a long, hard winter.

The oldest pub in Filey was The Ship. More affectionately known as T'Oard Ship, at the bottom of King Street (now Queen Street). T'Oard ship was a popular watering hole and licensed premises for two hundred years before confiscating its license. Subsequently, the pub closed on 1st October 1910. The T'Oard ship is forever romantically linked to the days of smuggling, which was rife in Filey and Scarborough.

At the pub's closing, newspaper reports state, 'The pub walls were three or four feet thick; hollow in places and used to store contraband. The beams in the great kitchen were simply a box with a sliding panel. A secret chamber in the adjoining cottage under the hearth was once the pub storeroom. The upstairs bedroom contained a double floor with peepholes commanding a complete range of Filey Bay.'

Shipwrecked sailors were taken to this pub for food and warmth throughout the years, and many a shiny gold coin had passed over the counter as salvage money to local fishermen.

Later in 1910, The Reverend Oxley of Petersham Vicarage, near Surrey, owned the adjoining cottage with its smuggler's hole – once a famous

haunt referred to by Charles Dickens and the author of the poem *T'*
Fisherfolk of Filey Bay. (This poem so interested Queen Victoria that she
asked for a copy to take to Balmoral.) Reverend Oxley purchased the
T'Oard Ship and other adjoining cottages to renovate them and turn the
buildings into a reading room, a smoking and writing room, and a
museum. He also intended to use the old pub as a fisherman's shelter
and outlook.

The pub's character was kept, with its famous blue Dutch tiles, and an
artist painted a fish over the mantel from days gone by. To this, other
people added the words:

'O ye whales and all that move in the water, bless ye, Lord,

praise him and magnify him forever.'

The signboard remained above the door. Underneath was the model of
a rigged ship, which in Yorkshire dialect said: 'They that go down to the
sea in ships and exercise their business in great waters. These men see
the works of the Lord for his wonders in the deep.' Then below the door:
'Oh that men would, therefore, praise the Lord for his goodness, and
declare the wonders that he doeth for children of men.'

T' Oard Ship (2017)

Next door to T'Oard Ship is The Foords. Originally named The New Inn, it was Filey's first purpose-built lodging house. One of the inn's first landlords was Mr Mosey, followed in 1814 by William Mason. The inn boasted it sold a large stock of genuine wines and spirituous liqueurs. The premises were also the pickup point for The Hull & Scarborough Express Company, which ran a daily coach express service to Scarborough. This service was the only means of transport to the neighbouring towns and villages. This coach left the New Inn at six in the morning, arriving at The Talbot Inn in Scarborough at two-thirty in the afternoon.

FOORD'S HOTEL, FILEY.

THE above old-established COMMERCIAL and FAMILY HOTEL is now replete with every convenience.

WELL-AIRED BEDS.

FINE OLD WINES, of the Finest Vintages.

BASS' PALE ALE, in Bottles and Small Casks.

MEUX'S STOUT, in Bottles and on Draught.

FAMILIES SUPPLIED AT WHOLESALE PRICES.

AN OMNIBUS ATTENDS EACH TRAIN.

CARRIAGES OF EVERY DESCRIPTION.

NEW INN, (late MOSEY's,)
FILEY.

WILLIAM MASON,
(Late Servant to Mrs. Bethell, of Rise,)

BEGS leave to acquaint the PUBLIC in general, that he has taken and entered upon the above well-known HOUSE:—which he has entirely new Furnished, and fitted up with every requisite for the comfort and convenience of those who please to visit this pleasant SEA-BATHING RETREAT.— He has also provided a Stock of the VERY BEST WINES, SPIRITS, &c.; to which, as well as to every other department of the House, it is his determination to pay the most particular attention: He therefore respectfully solicits the public support.

N. B. Commodious Bathing Machines, and careful Attendants, during the Season.

FILEY, April, 1814.

THOMAS FOORD,
NEW INN, FILEY,

BEGS to return his most sincere Thanks to the Nobility, Gentry, and the Public in general, for the liberal favours conferred upon him during his residence at the above Inn, and respectfully informs them, that he has added to his Concern, neat *Post Chaises and good Horses,* which, with care and attention, he hopes to merit a share of Business.

T. F. has also laid in a choice Stock of Old Wines and Spirits; and has fitted up his Beds in a superior Style, which enables him to render comfortable Accommodation to Families, Commercial Travellers, and others.

The Express Coach to and from Hull and Scarbro', every day, Sundays excepted.

Among the most popular licensees at The New Inn were Mr & Mrs Thomas Foord. Locals affectionately knew the pub by the host's surname: 'The Foords Hotel' or simply 'Foord's'. This name stuck. After that, the New Inn changed its name permanently to remember the town's popular licensees. Mr Foord died unexpectedly in 1839 of a seizure after stabling some horses in the coach house. Reports state that Dr Munroe's surgeon was called but could not revive Mr Foord. His widow later married a Mr Robinson from Ayton in 1845.

Foords Hotel (2016)

The Britannia

At 65-71, Queen Street was The Britannia pub. The pub's last licensee was Mr William Gutherless, who had run the pub for two years but had found the business very difficult. He stated this was because the premises were in a bad state of repair, and there was no stabling, rendering it unpopular with travellers. To make matters worse, the police charged Mr Gurtherless with keeping the premises open beyond its permitted licensing hours (a regular occurrence in Filey) and for serving the coastguard and his friends after time. Later the police dropped these as it transpired the coastguard was a friend of the Landlord. However, Mr Gurtherless could not sustain the business, and the pub's license was discontinued at the 1889 Brewster sessions.

Barrels waiting for collection outside The Britannia photograph courtesy Stephen Eblet

71 Queen Street – you can still see the outline of The Britannia pub

The Pack Horse Inn

OLD ESTABLISHED

PACK HORSE INN,

QUEEN STREET, FILEY.

WINES AND SPIRITS; ALE AND PORTER, BOTTLED AND DRAUGHT.

REFRESHMENTS ON THE SHORTEST NOTICE.

Horses and Carriages for hire. Good Coach-house and Stabling.

JOHN GIBSON, Proprietor.

The Pack Horse Inn was at 78 Queen Street, and its last landlady, Mrs Elizabeth Kilby, was a likeable and capable host. Elizabeth took the licence for The Pack Horse from John Gibson in 1875. Elizabeth's first husband, Henry John Kilby, died, aged 48 in 1874, leaving her a widow with three children to support. Henry had run The Foords but was declared bankrupt in 1869.

The Pack Horse Queen Street was built similarly to the old fisherman's cottages. It was demolished, and, in its place, came The Crown Hotel, a more prominent and modern hotel with additional boarding rooms and adequate stabling to accommodate Filey's ever-increasing stream of visitors. Mrs Kilby was the Crown's first licensee.

Perhaps, ill-advised, Elizabeth Kilby married William M Stubbs, a farmer from Cayton, in 1881. Business for the Stubbs did not go well. It is recorded in the Yorkshire Post/Leeds Intelligencer that just four years later, in 1885, Mr William Stubbs of Cayton, a farmer, cattle dealer and innkeeper of The Crown Hotel Filey, had substantial debts and was declared bankrupt. The police also charged Stubbs with being drunk on his premises and permitting drunkenness.

Following Stubbs's bankruptcy, a few things came to light. Elizabeth Kilby (Stubbs) had previously received a loan from her brother Thomas Wilson who had loaned her six hundred pounds plus interest to purchase The Pack Horse Inn. She subsequently married Stubbs. The Pack Horse was demolished, and The Crown Inn was erected. Elizabeth had since mortgaged the Crown Inn to Messrs.' Woodall & Hebden bankers in Scarborough, but Mr Wilson had not been repaid. After her marriage, her husband William came into possession of the Crown and all its furniture. Still, within the Women's Property Amendment Act provisions, a husband was not liable for his wife's debt before the marriage. As Stubbs had been declared bankrupt with many creditors seeking repayment of debts, Mr Wilson only received the sum of one hundred and fifty pounds plus court costs., which he had little chance of ever receiving.

Mr Stubbs was not honest, as his two brothers and sister again took him to court. Stubbs's father had a farm at Cayton. He died in 1872. William Stubbs was the executor, and the terms of the will stipulated that the farm must continue in business for the benefit of the family. In 1880, Stubbs got a valuation on the farm of one thousand three hundred and sixty pounds, a share to which his siblings were entitled. Unfortunately for them, William Stubbs was taken to court, as the family had not received a penny. The Judge remarked Stubbs had grossly mismanaged his affairs and those of his wife, Elizabeth. William Stubbs died in 1889, aged just thirty-eight.

Elizabeth died in 1895, aged sixty-five. She left two daughters, Emily Annie and Grace Elizabeth Kilby. Also, a son named Henry John Kilby emigrated to New Zealand in the late 1800s with his wife, Christina. Elizabeth is buried in St Oswald's churchyard, where her inscription reads 'The beloved wife of Henry John Kilby.' No mention of her subsequent marriage.

The Crown Hotel continued as a public house until 2010, when it was closed and demolished to make way for local housing.

The Crown Hotel – is closed and ready for demolition

The Grapes, Queen Street

Also, on Queen Street is The Grapes, whose landlord in 1877 was Mr William Smith. Mr Smith did not run the pub properly and, at the Brewster sessions in Bridlington, was given one week to quit and leave the premises. A week earlier, the police had charged him with permitting drunkenness on the premises. The pub's owner, Sergeant Winpenny, was not impressed and swiftly found a replacement. This pub sadly closed its doors in 2019.

On Church Street, just around the corner from Queen Street, was The Hope & Anchor, demolished in 1896 to make way for Laundry Hill. Mr West appearing at Bridlington Brewster sessions on behalf of the landlord, applied for the licence to be transferred to new premises, which were to be next door to the demolished Hope and Anchor. This new pub would be called The Station Hotel, aptly named to attract visitors from the trains from West Yorkshire and beyond.

The Imperial Vaults

On the other side of town on Hope Street is The Imperial Vaults, which back in the 1880s was known as The Imperial Bottling Stores. Mr W. G. Long was the proprietor. Mr Long brewed his own beer, bottled it and sold it to the public, and he was also the sole agent for the sale of J. Tetley & Son's celebrated Ales. Mr Long retired in 1881. The property was advertised for sale in The Yorkshire Post. The advertisement states that 'the premises at 6 &7 Hope Street comprise two dwelling houses, extensive wine cellars, a shop, a dram shop and back premises with yards. Mr Thomas Brunton, who ran the business under Brunton & Greaves Imperial Bottling Stores & Innkeeper, purchased the premises. However, the business was short-lived, and Mr Brunton is cited in the London Gazette as filing for bankruptcy in March 1892.

W. G. LONG,
WINE AND SPIRIT VAULTS,
AND
ALE AND PORTER STORES,
6, HOPE STREET,
FILEY.

SOLE AGENT FOR
J. TETLEY AND SON'S
CELEBRATED ALES,
LEEDS.
11

In 1893, Mr Bennet bought the premises and renamed The Imperial Vaults. Mr Bennet was the licensee but employed a manager, Mr Proudiouck, to oversee the everyday running of the pub. An incident relating to this management is reported in the Yorkshire Herald of 1893 when Mr Bennet appeared before Bridlington Magistrate's court for allowing drunkenness on his premises. Mr Bennet took great exception to this, insisting that it should have been the manager on trial and not his good self as he was not in possession. The magistrates quickly overruled this objection as Mr Bennet was the licence holder and the person responsible. The police entered the bar late at night and found two men asleep at the bar who appeared to be very drunk and 'senseless. Witnesses were called, who all denied that the men were drunk. Their defence was that the men were navvies working on the new sea wall and could not get lodgings, so they usually slept in the cement sheds. However, about thirty men had been allowed to stay at the Imperial Vaults. They were all given breakfast and the use of soap and towels whenever they needed them. The manager Mr Proudiouck stated that the two men in question were overtired and not drunk. The bench took considerable time deciding their verdict and fined Mr Bennet twenty shillings plus costs. Mr Bennet subsequently terminated Mr Proudiouck's employment.

The Three Tuns

Photograph credit Joanne Cammish

One of Filey's biggest pubs is The Three Tuns on Murray Street. The first licensee was Mr Robert Jones, who transferred his licence in 1868 to Mr William Barker, former landlord of The Britannia Inn, Queen Street. Mr Barker renamed the premises 'Barkers Commercial & Family Inn & Posting house,' advertising that the bar sold the best quality bottled ales and porter in prime condition. The advert also boasted that there was an omnibus to meet every train. Mr Barker and his family were also the subject of court action and appeared before Bridlington magistrates for assaulting Mr Morgan Medd, a man of dubious integrity. Mr Barker & his son accused Mr Medd, a horse-breaker, of robbing people, and a fight broke out in the smoking room of The Three Tuns. The Barkers were found guilty and were ordered to pay twenty shillings each plus costs.

WILLIAM BARKER,

LIVERY STABLE KEEPER,

COMMERCIAL & FAMILY INN & POSTING HOUSE,

"THREE TUNS INN,"

MURRAY, STREET, FILEY.

WINES AND SPIRITS

OF THE VERY BEST QUALITY.

BOTTLED ALE AND PORTER

IN PRIME CONDITION.

FAMILIES SUPPLIED ON ADVANTAGEOUS TERMS.

EXTENSIVE STABLING AND LOCK-UP COACH-HOUSES.

AN OMNIBUS TO MEET EVERY TRAIN.

EVERY ACCOMMODATION FOR DAY VISITORS.

Throughout the years, The Three Tuns (and other inns) were often used as an auction house to sell land and property throughout Filey. In 1887, Mr Cammish sold three cottages in Stockdale's Yard, which he claimed provided a good investment and rental return. The properties were occupied by Mr Cammish, Mr Baxter, Mr Sayers, and their respective families. In September 1944, an auction at The Three Tuns advertised three hundred and twenty-four thousand acres of land and buildings known as Church Cliff Farm. The prospectus states that the property has about two miles of sea frontage and is prime building land.

The Star Charity Pigeon Race 1920 (In aid of Scarborough Hospital)

In the late 1800s, The Star Inn on Mitford Street was under the ownership of the Bulmer family. The Bulmer family was large, and the brothers had quite a reputation for fighting each other. In 1877, brothers John & Charles Bulmer were the licensees. The brothers were not getting along despite running the business together. On 12th January 1877, a disturbance was reported to the police. When officers called to the premises, the brothers were fighting. John Bulmer had used a knife on his brother, intending to cause him harm. Police reported that there was glass all over and broken chairs and tables. In court, the bench decided the brothers were 'unfit' to hold a liqueur licence, and the couple were fined fifty pounds each and bound over to keep the peace. The magistrates withdrew the pub's licence, not allowing the pub to reopen until a suitably responsible person could be found. That suitable person was the couple's other brother, James, who was later charged with allowing drunkenness on his premises.

In 1906, the Derby News reported the strange death of a solicitor from Leeds who stayed at the Star Hotel, Filey. The man, Mr Herbert Armstrong, was found lying on the pavement outside the pub in his nightshirt, with scalp wounds, a broken jaw and elbow, and several cuts and bruises. It later transpired that the solicitor was a chronic alcoholic who had ridden his bike to Foxholes and, on his return, had fallen off the bike and sustained these fatal injuries.

There were reports that another pub would be built in Filey, and a Mr Dawson Britten of Hull applied for a licence. Mr Britten told magistrates that the pub would be called *The Prince of Wales* to be built near the railway station. Mr Britten assured the bench that he had purchased the land for three hundred and seventy-five pounds and that building work would begin shortly. However, it transpired that Mr Britten had only left a deposit of twenty pounds and had insufficient funds to complete the project. The application for a licence was refused.

Seth Gregory & The Belle Vue

The Royal Hotel, Belle Vue Street. (Then North Terrace) Now the site of The Three Tuns car park

In May 1854, The Hull Packet & East Riding Times reported that there had been a severe fire at the Royal Hotel, Filey. The whole east wing of the hotel was on fire, and valuable furniture belonging to Mr Gregory was destroyed. Mr Gregory, who had only recently taken over as the lessee of the hotel, was slightly injured in the fire and overcome by smoke. However, these injuries were not serious. Scarborough fire brigade attended and found out that the fire had started in the fire grate of the dining room, which was only three inches away from the hearthstone – so close that it set fire to the adjoining wood. The damage to the hotel and its furniture amounted to eight hundred pounds. Fortunately, Mr Gregory affected the hotel's insurance policy and insured the furniture ten days before the fire. The Royal Hotel was subsequently closed and demolished shortly afterwards.

Seth Gregory was originally from Hull and had moved to Filey with his wife, Mary, to run The Royal Hotel. Following the fire, he acquired substantial land on Belle Vue Terrace, and in 1858, The Belle Vue Hotel was built. An advertisement in the Hull Packet states, 'These houses are recently constructed and ready for visitors' reception, worthy for nobility, clergy and gentry, there is good stabling, coach houses and a generous supply of water.' The Belle Vue Hotel competed with the newly constructed hotels and boarding houses on The Crescent, especially Taylor's Hotel (Royal Crescent Court), which attracted royalty and landed gentry from all over the country.

The Belle Vue (Cliff Hotel)

In 1858, Seth Gregory applied for a drinks licence at Bridlington petty sessions. Initially, his application was not looked upon favourably and was opposed. The main reason for the disapproval was that Filey had two thousand residents. There were already ten licensed premises, which the bench considered sufficient for a small town. It was also questioned that The Belle Vue was, in fact, three separate houses with separate entrances, and the bench was unsure of Mr Gregory's intentions. Did he want to cover all three houses or as one house under one licence? The chairman stipulated that he did not want to give a monopoly to one person. However, if Mr Gregory occupied the premises and the hotel had one entrance (for licensing purposes), they would grant a licence. The Belle Vue Hotel got its first 'On licence' on 23rd October 1858.

Seth Gregory did not intend to run the hotel himself, or he was finding the business harder than he expected, as, on 26th November 1858, an advert appeared in The Hull Packet & East Riding Times, saying. 'To let – recently constructed hotel, 70 rooms, the hotel may be entered immediately. The rent will begin on 6th April 1859, allowing the tenant to select his beers, wines and spirits. The advertisement also said, 'the present proprietor is retiring from the business.'

In December 1861, only four years after opening his hotel, a notice appeared in The London Gazette. The information required Mr Seth Gregory of Filey, in the county of York, the innkeeper, dealer and Chapman, to surrender himself to the official receivers and registrars of Leeds Crown Court, where he had been adjudged bankrupt. Seth could not compete with the affluent hotels on The Crescent, and his dream of running a high-class hotel overlooking the German Ocean ended.

On Friday, 26th September 1862, by order of the mortgagees and assignees of Seth Gregory, The Belle Vue, land and outbuildings were sold by public auction in separate lots. Seth left Filey with his wife, Mary, and returned to Hull, where he died shortly afterwards.

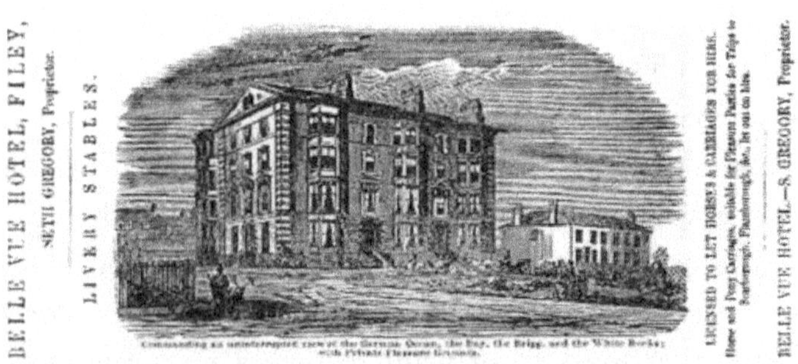

Filey's Hotels and Boarding Houses

Taylors' Crescent Hotel (now Royal Crescent Court & Bonhommes Bar)

Continuing our journey into Filey's social life, we concentrate on Filey's boarding houses and hotels.

With the Industrial Revolution, Victorian England brought many changes, including railways and the transformation of villages from small farming communities to bustling towns and cities. For the first time in

England, the censuses provided an accurate record of the number of inhabitants of each community, together with their occupations. In 1801, the census recorded the population of Filey to be 505. Following improvements in living conditions, including lighting, sewerage, and drainage, the population of Filey increased dramatically.

In the 1830s, Birmingham solicitor John Wilkes Unett (1770-1856) bought seven acres of land in Filey. Unett had a vision for Filey and employed the renowned architect Charles Edge to make his vision a reality. Filey was then transformed into a desirable and fashionable seaside resort attracting visitors from all over the country.

In 1854, Edwin Taylor moved from The Royal Hotel on Belle Vue Street to The Crescent Hotel, which took pride and place at the centre of the newly built elegant Crescent. He immediately renamed it

'Taylor's Crescent Hotel'. His terms were reasonable, as advertised in the Hull Packet in 1854.

Terms at Taylor's Crescent Hotel

Board & Lodging in Public Room – 6s

Ditto in Private Room – 7s

Table D' Hote' at Five o'clock. The above includes Attendance, Billiard Table and Bathrooms in the Hotel, Hot Sea-Water Baths, 2s, Shower, 1s. An omnibus and carriage meet all the Trains, good stabling and Coach Houses.

The hotel was finished to an opulent standard and considered one of the finest terraces in England. The hotel attracted the aristocracy and even royalty. The Guestlist of 1858 boasts visitors, such as

Their Royal Highnesses, the Grand Duke and Duchess of Hesse, and servants.

Her Royal Highness, the Princess Louise of Battenberg, and servants.

The Hon. GW Winn and Mrs of Walton Hall, Wakefield.

And many more.

The Crescent Gardens were a place of considerable beauty and provided musical entertainment throughout the season. Advertisements for musicians would appear in fashionable London magazines such as 'The Era,' looking for talented people to play in the bandstand in the Crescent gardens for summer. There was a small charge for entrance to the Gardens, and the original safe used for this purpose is in the basement at Bonhommes (Royal Crescent Court), where it will remain for a long time because of its weight and size.

The Crescent remains a very fashionable address. Taylors Crescent Hotel (now Royal Crescent Court) became privately owned apartments in 1965, together with the popular award-winning Bonhommes Bar, which has survived as the last business still operating on The Crescent.

The Hotel contains about 100 Rooms, comprising large Dining Room and Drawing Room for Ladies and Gentlemen, a Coffee Room for Gentlemen, Sitting Rooms, Bed Rooms, Billiard Room, Smoke Room, and Bath Rooms, &c., &c.

The White Lodge (South Crescent Villa)

South Crescent Villa-now The White Lodge Hotel 1912

At the end of The Crescent stands The White Lodge Hotel. Built in 1860, South Crescent Villa (as it was initially known) was a private house belonging to Colonel Ackroyd and his wife from Halifax, West Yorkshire. The Villa suffered a severe chimney fire in 1874, causing severe damage to the roof. Colonel Ackroyd sold the property shortly after the fire to actress Madge Kendal (later Dame) and her husband. They renamed the house 'Kendal house'.

The Kendals at Filey 1912

Mrs Kendal was born in Grimsby, the youngest of twenty-two children. The Kendal's travelled the world treading the boards and had five children. Reports suggest that Madge Kendal was a very cold lady, unable to separate her personal life from her acting career. She became estranged from all her children. When she died at her home in Hertfordshire in 1935, not one of her five children attended her funeral. Kendal House and all its contents were left solely to Miss Marie Lohr, an actress from Australia; the Kendal children got nothing.

As the years progressed and Filey became a major fashionable tourist resort, private lodging houses and hotels on The Crescent emerged. Mrs Barker was well recommended at no 23 The Crescent, offering a dining room and four bedrooms for four guineas a week. Mrs Knaggs on Belle Vue Street and Melville Place were also highly recommended. In 1939, Mr Wilson bought the buildings known as The Hylands Retirement Home, advertising it as 'Filey's newest hotel' offering access to tennis courts, gardens and all 'mod cons.' Hylands attracted many celebrities doing the rounds at Butlin's or Scarborough. Diana Dors stayed there, as did The Beatles in 1963 and 1964, after playing at The Futurist in Scarborough.

The Victoria Hotel was also a popular place for esteemed visitors. In 1937, Mrs Coracan, the hotel owner, applied to the police for a licence to hold dances for her customers throughout winter, something she had done regularly throughout summer. Neighbour Mrs Gofton objected to the noise and opposed the licence application. Subsequently, the justices agreed with Mrs Gofton and declined the application

Dancing was all the rage at The Pavilion Theatre (Southdene, now Sea Cadets). Andie Caine, the famous Pierrot, held many performances there, and the theatre became a popular dancing hall until its closure in the 1970s. The Grand Theatre (now The Buccaneer) was also a visitor's trendy place. Many performances were enjoyed there until it later became a cinema. In 1911, Filey tradesmen enjoyed a Christmas afternoon exhibition at the Grand Theatre when a mysterious fire started in the boiler room, and several shavings caught fire. Had it not been for the prompt action of Filey's fire brigade, the building would not be here today and would most likely have been yet another block of flats.

Pavilion Theatre (Now Filey Sea Cadets)

One of the best memories of Filey as a child is at Filey Sun Lounge, which hosted guests doing 'rounds' of summer, usually on their way back from Butlin's. The talent contests were terrific, and I remember practising singing along in my bedroom, using a hairbrush as a microphone. I never won, but I remember a girl from Doncaster winning one year. She had a lovely voice and was called Elizabeth Taylor – unfortunately, not the same one. Ken Goodwin was a popular favourite, with his brilliant catchphrase 'settle down now', a lovely, sensitive, funny and professional man and entertainer, sadly missed.

Butlin's Filey closed in 1984. Its closure devastated the town's tourist industry and many Filey businesses that supplied goods to the camp, such as the local dairy, greengrocers and Filey laundry. Yet, Filey remains a popular holiday resort thanks to the dedication of the landlords/landladies and hotel and boarding house owners who work incredibly hard all year. Credit to them all.

Coroners Inquests & Trials & Petty Sessions

Charles Dickens declared, 'The Coroner frequents more public houses than any man alive.' He wasn't wrong, as, in the 18th and 19th centuries, Inns and public houses were central to the administration of local justice before the formation of the police courts and offered an additional source of income to the landlord with increased trade and thirsty spectators wanting to sit in the sessions and fuel their curiosity. The public houses in Filey had their fair share of inquests and petty sessions throughout the years. Here are just a few together with court sessions.

1640

Stephen Martin of Filey appeared at York Castle, where he was described as a dangerous rogue, work-shy, a wanderer and a burglar and was branded on the left shoulder with the letter R.

1863

A Coroner's inquest was held before Mr ED Conyers at The Packhorse Inn upon the body of nine-year-old Sarah Anne Bullamore. The child's mother sent her on an errand, and whilst crossing the road where there was a sharp turn, a horse and cart driven by the son of Mr Prust, a butcher from Muston, struck the child, and she died instantly. A verdict of accidental death was recorded.

1871

The assistant coroner, Mr W.M. Wigmore, held an inquest at The Pack Horse on the body of a badly decomposed sailor on Filey Brigg. The sailor was one of the crew of the ill-fated Unico. In January 1871, the Unico crashed on the Brigg. A verdict of 'Found Drowned' was recorded. At the funeral, great respect was shown, and the coffin was wrapped with the ship's colours and followed to the grave by Captain Huntley and Mr Cook, overseer of the town's poor and many local tradesmen.

Flying

The broad cliffs and vast sands of Filey attracted amateur aviators from all over the country. Thus, in May 1910, permission was granted by Filey Urban District Council to Mr J. W. F. Tranmer of Scarborough to use Filey sands for aviation training. Mr Tranmer erected a hangar and bungalow at Primrose Valley, together with a twelve-foot-wide slipway, constructed to facilitate the winching of aircraft down to the beach 60 yards below. Two 25 h.p Bleriot monoplanes were brought over from France and delivered to Filey by rail, and a flying school was opened nearby.

Blackburn Maiden Flight. Credit John M. Smith.

The first recorded flight from Filey beach was on 25th July 1910 by Bradford man Mr William House, a member of the Northern Aero syndicate. Mr House had planned his first Filey flight to coincide with his honeymoon. However, this flight was not entirely successful as he smashed the plane's wing and ended up soaked in petrol and trapped in the wreckage. It took several local people some time to extract him from the plane. Not the best way to start a marriage.

Mr Tranmer lost interest in his enterprise as he advertised the property for rent in-Flight magazine. Subsequently, Mr Robert Blackburn rented the premises and renamed it Blackburn Flying School. Mr Blackburn was originally from Leeds and is credited as one of the first pioneers of British Aviation. One of Blackburn's flying instructors was Essex-born Mr Bentfield Charles Hucks, who learned to fly on Filey beach.

Early in 1911, a prize of fifty pounds was offered for the first pilot to fly between Filey and Leeds. Hucks made several attempts at this but was unsuccessful. In June 1911, he had a serious accident when flying between Filey and Scarborough when the propeller of his plane fell off. The plane lurched forward and crashed headfirst onto Filey beach. Mr

Hucks sustained injuries to his head and legs, and some spectators received minor injuries, but the plane was a complete right off.

In December 1911, another instructor of the Blackburn Flying school was Mr Hubert Oxley. With his assistant 32-year-old Robert Weiss, a rag-merchant from Dewsbury, he flew to Leeds in his 'Mercury' plane to win the fifty-pound prize. Before setting off to Leeds, Mr Oxley took a preliminary flight around Filey. The weather was clear, with a slight frost in the air. Scores of spectators had lined the beach to watch the flight, which was a success until Oxley descended on the beach just in front of the lifeboat shed. The plane was about 80 feet when suddenly it buckled backwards, and the machine dived onto the sands. Mr Oxley was shot head-first out of his seat like a projectile, landing 15 yards away on his head. He didn't stand a chance. His neck was broken, and death was instantaneous.

Robert Weiss was unconscious and pinned under the plane. His injuries were severe, including a fractured skull, broken thighs, ankles, and internal injuries. He was taken to the coastguard station, where he died shortly after.

A spokesperson for Filey stated that Mr Oxley had intended to take as a passenger his engineer Mr A. C. Hunt, who was already seated on the plane when Mr Weiss appeared, asking to be allowed on the flight. Mr Oxley had reluctantly agreed. At the inquest, Mr Hunt gave an engineer's statement that Mr Oxley was fond of diving with his engine working instead of volplaning. Mr Hunt said that when he accompanied him on one occasion, he had warned Mr Oxley that he was looking for trouble, but Mr Oxley had just laughed!

The tragic deaths did not deter aviators, who continued their quest to fly between Leeds and Filey. Mr Brereton, a pilot from Bristol, replaced Mr Oxley, who, with the engineer, Mr Hunt, attempted to win the Royal Aero Club pilot certificate. Two new planes were purchased, including a Blackburn monoplane fitted with an improved Isaacson engine; they were housed in the hangar on Primrose Valley.

Credit Philip Gibson

In 1912, the Blackburn Flying School sent a letter to Filey Urban Council, stating that owing to the expense of keeping machines at Filey and the lack of any financial support from the town. The company advised that it would have to move to another county. The company asked the council if it would consider subsidising the cost of the hangar expenses. It would continue with its experiments with a hydroplane in Filey Bay and conduct the trials of its new military machines. The company argued that if Filey remained an aviation centre, it would significantly benefit the town.

The council decided it could be of no help as a public body. Mr Blackburn moved his operation to Hendon in September 1912.

1916 saw the Blackburn & Aeroplane Motor Company move to Brough (Near Hull), where it built a new factory. Through the war years, the company flourished, especially with the proximity of the Humber, which was ideal for launching seaplanes. The company continued to grow and, in 1939, became Blackburn Aircraft Ltd. By 1949. The company is amalgamated with General Aircraft Ltd. In 1955, this company won a contract to supply new aircraft to the Royal Navy. The plane, the NA39, known as The Buccaneer, was very successful and was in production for twenty years. In 1960, the company became The Hawker Blackburn division of the giant Hawker Siddeley Aviation Combine, which in 1965 became Hawker Siddeley (Brough) and later became part of the British Aerospace Kingston-Brough Division.

The aircraft hangar at Primrose Valley was initially used for storage by the military battalions engaged in coastal defence duties. The hangar was sold in 1921 to Mr Frederick Parker, an engineer from Hunmanby, who dismantled it to house his tractor engines. Unfortunately, the hangar was not fit for this purpose and was re-sold.

The dismantling of the Hangar. Credit Philip Gibson.

Filey is credited with having a significant influence on the aviation industry. Mr Hubert Hucks was acknowledged as the first pilot in England to loop the loop. On 25th July 1914, Hucks flew over Hunmanby and completed the Filey railway station roof loop. A plaque has been erected on the seafront to commemorate Filey's involvement in flying.

Dr Edward William Pritchard

Dr Edward William Pritchard. Artist Gareth Jenkinson.

© W M Rhodes.

Edward Pritchard was born in Southsea, a small seaside town near Portsmouth, on 6th December 1825, to a respectable naval family.

He claimed to have studied medicine at Kings College London, from where he alleges he graduated in 1846. (There are no records of his qualifying from this college). More likely, he purchased a venal certificate from Erlangen, Germany.

Pritchard served in the Royal Navy as an assistant surgeon on Nelson's ship at the battle of Trafalgar, HMS Victory. He then sailed worldwide on various ships, eventually returning to Portsmouth, where he met his future wife, Mary Jane Taylor, the daughter of Michael Taylor, a prosperous silk merchant from Glasgow. The couple married in 1851 and had five children.

After serving in the Navy, Pritchard became a General Doctor in Hunmanby, near Filey. Pritchard kept a summer hour at Clarence Place, Filey, and a part share of a doctor's surgery on West Road. Pritchard was not a popular figure in Filey. He was known for cheating with his female patients and embellishing the truth. He would also ride his horse into All Saints' Church Hunmanby, much to the annoyance of the congregation.

Betty Chandler, a widow from Hunmanby, died under suspicious circumstances. Pritchard was responsible, but there was no proof and the rumours faded.

Pritchard was known for writing a visitor's guide to Filey. He also lectured on his many (often disputed) travels worldwide at the Mechanics Institute on Belle Vue Street. Pritchard was also present at Taylors Crescent Hotel's opening, and he was also present when Roman artefacts were found on Carr Naze. As an arrogant, selfish man, he always needed to be on the frontline of Filey's hierarchy. Pritchard left Filey under a cloud. Rumour was he was flirting with too many other men's wives. The adulterous doctor was no longer welcome in Filey.

He and his family left Filey in 1859 and moved to the fashionable Berkeley Street, Glasgow. In May 1863, a severe fire at Pritchard's house killed twenty-five-year-old Elizabeth McGrain (Lizzy). Much controversy surrounded her death. Lizzy did not escape, suggesting that she was possibly unconscious, drugged, or dead. The Insurance company suspected Pritchard's claim and refused to pay. Despite the police discovering that the door to Lizzy's room was locked from the outside, they did not pursue any criminal charges. The inquest assumed Lizzy had been reading in bed next to a jet flame that ignited the bed sheets, and Lizzy suffocated.

In 1864, just after the family had moved to Sauchiehall Street, Mary Jane Pritchard fell ill. Mary Jane's mother came from Edinburgh to look after her. She also fell ill and died aged seventy. A month later, Mary Jane died aged thirty-eight.

Following an anonymous letter to the Procurator Fiscal in Glasgow, Pritchard was arrested. Both women's bodies were exhumed and found traces of antimony poison were in their bodies.

Pritchard stood trial for murder in July 1865. The jury took just half an hour to find him guilty, and he was sentenced to death by hanging.

He faced the gallows at Jail Square in Glasgow just before Nelson's column on 28th July 1865. A crowd of one hundred thousand people witnessed the poisoning practitioner's demise.

Pritchard was the last man to be hanged publicly in Scotland. After this, all executions were carried out behind prison walls, away from the brutal glee of the public.

If you visit Filey surgery, you can see a picture on the wall of Dr Edward William Pritchard and be grateful that Filey had the sense to banish this man, or Filey could have been famous for these most prolific Victorian murders.

The Pritchard Family. Author's Collection.

Accidents & Murders

The Fall of Three Young Men

Between the years 1862 and 1909. Three young Filey men fell to their deaths in different circumstances.

On the afternoon of 8th October 1862, fifteen-year-old Thomas Henry Suggitt, the son of Thomas and Zillah Suggitt (nee Agar), was on Filey Brigg, where he often searched for objects for his hobby as a nature lover.

This afternoon he was searching for artefacts for his sister's aquarium. Thomas was a well-respected and educated young man who had just secured a place at a London College to study civil engineering.

Thomas was last seen alive, heading towards the cliffs on the north side. He would have climbed up the ridge, a frequently used but difficult mountain-like pathway. A dangerous part of the cliff is the 'neck' aptly named and is just wide enough to give a foothold, albeit very treacherous. The best way to pass the 'neck' was to take a quick sprint. Thomas, it seemed, had succeeded with this deathly dash and ascended to an altitude of approximately fifty feet and tried to position his collection boxes higher up the cliff when he lost his footing and fell backwards. Thomas rolled from ridge to ridge and tried desperately to regain his hold; unfortunately, he lost his grip and fell over the edge to the rocks below. Shortly afterwards, his body was found, and reports confirmed that death occurred instantly.

Amos Proctor was born in Muston in April 1848. He was one of eight children born to Thomas Proctor and Sarah (nee Edmund.) The Proctors were a notorious family, and Amos was the twin brother of the iniquitous Maria Proctor (Stonehouse). She was bludgeoned to death by her drunken, violent husband, Samuel Stonehouse, in Filey in 1894.

Amos's mother, Sarah, was also no stranger to crime. She had appeared in front of the judge at Bridlington petty sessions in 1867 for stealing a pair of men's boots belonging to Mr Thomas Vasey of Filey and received a twenty-pound fine.

In 1870 Amos worked at J & E Jacques Flour mill in Scarborough. Amos had gone to the upper storey of the mill to attach the strap to the revolving 'sack tackle' when he got himself jammed between the upright shaft and the revolving apparatus. A colleague quickly tried to raise the alarm and shut the power off. Amos was eventually freed and taken to his home in Muston, where despite the best efforts of Dr Taylor, the local GP, Amos died in the early hours of the following morning, aged just twenty-two. The inquest recorded a verdict of accidental death when it transpired that Amos had attempted to put the strap on the four-wheel with his foot.

Amos's sister, the unfortunate Maria, could not accept the death of her beloved twin brother, which is most likely the reason for her rapid decline and her life spiralling out of control. It might explain why she turned to drink, a significant contribution to her eventual murder. (See a Scandalous Woman)

*

John Rawson was the youngest son of William and Elizabeth Ann Rawson nee Maulson, who lived at 32, Queen Street, Filey.

Aged nineteen, John worked as a plumber for Councillor Gibson. On 20th May 1909, Mr Gibson had sent John and a colleague Mr Lindley to a job at 3 Belle Vue, Filey, a property belonging to Dr and Mrs Croke of Hull. John had done various jobs for the Croke's in the past, and they were very fond of him, and Mrs Croke had specifically requested Mr Gibson to send John, as he had recently fitted some gas fittings for her and general maintenance. On a fateful evening, Mrs Croke asked if John could clean her windows.

John was used to heights and climbed onto the V-shaped ledge. Unfortunately, he lost his footing and fell off the ledge onto his arm, then his head, cracking his skull on the pavement. John was taken to his sister's house, Mrs Webb, at 2 Rutland Terrace, but he did not regain consciousness despite some hope.

An inquest was held on the 28th of May 1909, which recorded a verdict of accidental death. No blame attached to anyone, just a stern warning of the dangers of cleaning windows at such a dangerous height.

A Scandalous Woman

Maria Proctor was born in Muston in 1848; she was the fourth of eight children born to Thomas Proctor and Sarah Edmund. Maria had a twin brother, Amos, who died in an industrial accident whilst working for R & B Jacques flour mill in Scarborough in 1870.

Maria had an illegitimate son, Thomas William Proctor, when she met Samuel Stonehouse from Scalby. The couple married in 1878 and rented a seventy-two-acre farm at Low Moor, Hunmanby, from Mrs Dale, Scarborough. Samuel and Maria had three more children, Ellen Elizabeth, Samuel Dixon, and Sarah. Ellen Elizabeth died in February 1889 at age ten.

Samuel was a quiet, hard-working man, but when he and Maria started drinking, which they often did, their quarrelling and fights were notorious. Neither were strangers to the Bridlington petty sessions, and both appeared before the judge in 1878 on entirely different charges. Samuel (milk-seller) received a fine of one pound plus costs for using a horse in an unfit state – the poor horse fell twice whilst attempting to draw a bathing machine out of the sea. Maria (milk-seller) appeared later in the same year for watering milk down by ten per cent and was fined two pounds plus twelve shillings' costs. This misdemeanour could explain why they moved to Filey, ending at a small cottage off Queen Street at the end of Barnett's Yard.

Samuel and Maria's drunken arguments were a regular occurrence, and Maria's screams of 'murder' were often heard when she took a battering off Samuel. Maria did her fair share of the battling, and the couple's landlord, John Barnett, referred to Maria as the worst of the two and called her a 'scandalous woman'. Maria could match Samuel with drinking, and many times Samuel would hand most of his wages to Maria on Saturday afternoon, but by Sunday evening, it was all gone.

On Saturday, 27th October 1894, Samuel worked as a bricklayer's labourer, erecting new buildings next to the Spa Saloon. He called into the Imperial Vaults on Hope Street with friends at lunchtime. Maria soon came looking for him, knowing that Samuel had collected his wages; she wanted her share so she could also go out drinking. Samuel and Maria continued drinking in the pubs of Filey, and Samuel was so intoxicated in The Star that the barman refused to serve him any more alcohol. In the meantime, a reasonably sober Maria went home to do some baking.

When Samuel eventually went home to Barnett's Yard, the fighting started. The couple's two children, Sarah and Samuel Dixon, were present, and the neighbours took no notice of throwing pots and pans – a regular occurrence at the Stonehouse's on a Saturday night. Samuel Dixon became increasingly concerned when he witnessed his father striking his mother across the head with a firebrick. The brick split in two and fractured Maria's skull. Samuel Dixon ran to fetch his uncle Edmund. Edmund returned with Sergeant Clarkson, who witnessed Maria lying on the sofa, moaning, 'Oh my poor body, he has kicked me to death.' Blood was flowing from the wound at the back of her head, and she had broken her arm trying to defend herself from Samuels's blows. Dr Orr, the local doctor, attended, but it was too late. Maria, aged 46, died from her wounds shortly afterwards. Samuel was subsequently arrested and taken into custody at Hull jail for the murder of his wife.

In November 1894, Samuel Stonehouse stood trial at York assizes. A post-mortem on Maria revealed she had a diseased heart and liver, and despite thirty-nine wounds on Maria's body, the court doctor, Dr Stephens, reported that Maria had died of shock. The couple's children, who were now in the custody of their uncle Edmond, said their mother drank. The judge and jury considered this evidence, convicted Samuel of the lesser charge of manslaughter and sentenced him to fourteen years of penal servitude. Samuel Stonehouse wrote to the Secretary of State to appeal his sentence. The facts were considered, along with many letters praising Samuel's previous good character. Hence, his sentence was reduced to twelve years.

When released from prison, Samuel returned to his hometown of Scarborough and died in 1920 at age seventy-two.

Five Children Drowned on Reighton Sands

Credit Ian Nisbet

In October 1902, Mr Luke White, coroner, held an inquest on the bodies of four of the five children swept away by the tide at Reighton, Filey, whilst they were playing on the sands. In his opening statement, Mr White said it was one of the most painful inquests he had ever had to conduct. A great disaster had fallen upon not only the parents of these poor unfortunate children, but a veil of sadness had encompassed the whole town. On Friday afternoon (August 1902), these young girls were playing on the beach enjoying themselves, when shortly after, they were all lying dead in the same cottage they were previously staying. A harrowing scene for all involved. Every attempt was made to save these children.

Credit Ian Nisbet

Mrs Lavinia Taylor, the mother of three girls, had lost her entire family. She had been visiting her husband's sister, Mrs Webster, who lived in a cottage at Reighton Gap. Mrs Taylor had stayed a fortnight and was due to go home to Leeds the day before, but the children had insisted they stay a little longer. The cousins were habitually going onto the sand and digging sandcastles.

Credit Ian Nisbet

On Friday, 29th August, the girls had made a sandcastle, taken off their boots and stockings, and had a paddle in the water. Three-year-old Hannah Mary Webster was reluctant to paddle, but her cousin, nine-year-old Clarissa, persuaded her, saying, 'come on, don't be a baby. We're having fun!' Five minutes later, the five children were surrounded by water; frightened, they screamed. Hearing the screams, the mothers saw the dangerous position of their daughters and at once threw off their boots and attempted to reach and rescue them. One mother went almost up to her neck in the water. Unfortunately, when she found the water was carrying her away, she was forced to relinquish her attempt. The mother's frantic screams alerted Miss Harper, who knew the sands and quickly took off her dress and jumped into the sea to rescue the girls, but again, to no avail. Mr Cass, a violinist from Scarborough, tried to save the girls, but before he could get to them, he went underneath the water and had no choice but to save himself. Screams were heard from the children as a giant wave engulfed them and carried them all off together. The last sight was the girls' heads bobbing up and down, then no trace of them.

The five children were:

Martha Alice Webster, 11

Hannah Mary Webster, 3

Their cousins, daughters of David and Lavinia Taylor of Kirkland Place, Beeston, Leeds.

Lillian Taylor 12

Elsie Taylor 7

Clarissa Taylor 9

The part of the beach where the children drowned was almost deserted. Nobody appeared to have noticed that the children were in danger in time to save them.

The coroner did not find it necessary to record any further evidence and praised the mothers, Miss Harper and Mr Cass, for their conduct and bravery. The coroner and the jury expressed their heartfelt sympathy to the bereaved parents, and he recorded a verdict of accidental drowning.

R.I.P Little Girls-You are not forgotten.

Credit Ian Nisbet

The Ardlamont Mystery and Filey's Connection to Sherlock Holmes

AJ Monson. The Sketch 1893.

Filey district has a connection to Sherlock Holmes and the beginnings of forensic science. The link begins with Alfred John Monson, born in 1860, the son of Rev. Thomas John Monson and Caroline Isabella Monckton, daughter of the 5th Viscount Galway. The fifth Viscount Galway discontinued the use of the surname of Arundel by Royal licence in 1826 and instead got permission for each successive holder of the title and his eldest son to use the surname Monckton-Arundel while the younger branches of the family should use Monckton only.

Alfred John Monson was the tenth child of twelve children. Born at Bedale, John married Agnes Maude Day in 1881, the daughter of William George Day, from Eversley, Yorkshire. The couple married in South Africa but returned to Yorkshire soon after.

In 1891, Mr Pilling occupied Gristhorpe Hall, Filey. A moderately sized country house. Mr Pilling wanted to travel abroad and agreed to let the hall go to Mr & Mrs Monson. Mrs Monson immediately placed an advert in the local paper for a good plain cook and a nursemaid for her children.

Gristhorpe Hall. Credit Crimlisk/Fisher Archives.

The couple set down to county life with their five children. (The Monson's had seven children) Their fifth child Violet Theodosia was born in Gristhorpe and christened at St Oswald's Parish Church, Filey.

Thirty-two-year-old Monson had been in and out of financial difficulties for most of his adult life. He was introduced to the Hambrough family in London and secured the job as gentleman's tutor to twenty-year-old Captain Windsor Dudley Cecil Hambrough (known as Cecil).

The Hambrough family seat was Pipewell Hall, Northamptonshire. Together with Steephill, Isle of Wight. The Hambrough's employed

Monson as their son's gentleman tutor. The dashing young lieutenant lived with the Monson family at Gristhorpe Hall. Another close friend, Captain Cowan or Cowen, was a frequent guest. There was a time when the three men were inseparable, going on many fishing trips and shooting expeditions around Gristhorpe Hall.

The Monson family were popular within the Filey and Gristhorpe community. In July 1891, the family attended Filey Parish Church, where Hambrough stood as godfather to one of Monson's children. All the Monson family had many dealings with the Filey and Scarborough businessmen. Caroline Isabella Monson, Monson's mother, lived on the South Cliff at Scarborough, where she was a popular figure in aristocratic life. She was once a lady-in-waiting for the Duchess of Edinburgh. Viscount Oxenbridge was Monson's uncle and the Dowager Lady Galway, his aunt.

The family lived in Gristhorpe for eighteen months before Mr Pilling returned from his travels. The couple then moved to Riseley Hall, Ripley, Yorkshire, when Monson's financial troubles came to the forefront.

In 1893, he took the lease on the Ardlamont estate in Argyll for the shooting season. His pupil, twenty-year-old Windsor Dudley Cecil Hambrough, joined him; he had lived with Monson, his wife and three children at Risley Hall. The 640-acre Ardlamont Estate is a chunk of spectacularly beautiful Argyll countryside, bordering the Kyles of Bute and close to the village of Tighnabruaich. On 10 August 1893, Monson took Hambrough, his pupil, for a day's hunting in an area of woodland on the estate.

Ardlamont House. Illustrated London News 1893.

Rumours suggest that twenty-year-old Hambrough had had an illicit relationship with Mrs Monson. On 10 August, Monson took Hambrough on a day's hunting in an area of woodland. A third man joined them, Edward Scott, a friend of Monson (who claimed to be a boating engineer. Although he had an alias, Edward Sweeney or Ted Davis). Scott had arrived at the estate a few days earlier.

On 10 August 1893. Monson and Scott took Hambrough on a day's hunting in an area of the estate's woodland. Moments later, estate workers heard a shot. When Monson and Scott returned to the estate, the butler found them both cleaning their guns when asked what had happened to young Mr Hambrough. Monson replied he had accidentally shot himself in the head while climbing a fence. However, as Hambrough was shot in the back of the head, although he was visibly upset by the young man's untimely death, Monson soon became the prime suspect on a charge of murder.

Lieutenant Hambrough 1893

The authorities reported the incident, and the <u>Inveraray procurator fiscal</u>'s office attended to the estate. He returned, saying it had been a tragic accident. There was not any formal post-mortem. However, a couple of weeks later, it came to the attention of the Procurator Fiscal that just days before his death, Cecil had insured his life for £2,000 only six days before Hambroughs's death and assigned the policies to Mrs Monson. The Monson's were now trying to collect. The Procurator Fiscal investigated further and found some evidential inconsistencies and that Monson was at the centre of a complex web of dodgy financial dealings involving the Hambrough family. And the mysterious 'Scott', who had shown no evidence of being a boating engineer, had disappeared. The Procurator Fiscal and the Crown decided that neither the shooting nor the boating incident the day before were accidents and charged Monson and Scott with murder and attempted murder.

Soon after, rumours circulated about Monson's financial difficulties. Mrs Monson had received a debt recovery summons from a lady's tailor in Glasgow. The sheriff dismissed the case in court. The law prohibited a wife from being sued for an account in her name. Her husband should take responsibility. Mr Monson had many financial troubles. It came to light that he was an undisclosed bankrupt, and now that his employer and meal ticket were dead, his financial difficulties increased. Monson had tried to raise loans through money lenders. The police and insurance company questioned Monson, who said the policy was in Mrs Monson's name as she had a separate estate, and Hambrough was too young to affect his own life. It emerged that upon Hambrough coming of age (his twenty-first birthday), he would inherit two hundred thousand pounds—a colossal amount of money in those days.

The insurance company did not complete the policy as they were unsatisfied with the arrangements. Monson persevered, and the day before his ward's untimely death, the Insurance company said they would affect a reduced insurance policy subject to proof of an insurable influence. Hambrough's death prevented the contract from completing.

The deceased's body was exhumed, but at this stage, all evidence was purely circumstantial. A few bullets were found by the tree where the dead man fell. There was concern over the position of the fatal shot, but nothing conclusive.

At one-thirty the day before, a boating accident involving the same three men had occurred. Monson had hired a boat, which had hit a rock, filled with water and sank. Unfortunately, Hambrough could not swim. Monson swam ashore and fetched another boat to rescue his ward. On this occasion, Hambrough's life was saved.

The murder case went to trial at the High Justice of Justiciary in December 1893 before Lord Justices Clerk Lord Kingsborough. The trial was a media frenzy. *The Illustrated London News* was already stating that it 'will certainly be one of the celebrated criminal trials of the century (December 9, 1893). The large-scale and unsuccessful manhunt for 'Scott', now believed to be Edward Sweeney, also known as Ted Davis, the bookmaker, had also captured the public's imagination and lent an air of mystery to the case.

Following the publicity, Scott, alias Edward Sweeney, and Davies, known in racing circles as Long Ted, gave himself up to the Pall Mall Gazette Office. He was taken to Scotland Yard and sent back to Scotland.

Over one hundred pressmen attended the trial, and *The Scotsman* devoted an average of twenty columns daily to it. Experts suggest that today, it would be an open-and-shut case, especially with the sort of testimony the prosecution called to the stand.

Among the witnesses for the prosecution was Joseph Bell, the Edinburgh surgeon and forensic detective. The author of the Sherlock Holmes adventures, Arthur Conan Doyle, met Bell in 1877 and served as his clerk at the Edinburgh Royal Infirmary. Bell was his mentor, teacher, and friend and was famous among students for his incredible powers of deduction. Bell could look at patients and diagnose them based on their appearance and demeanour. The prototype for the fictional character was Bell.

Bell told the jury that, in his opinion, Monson had murdered Cecil Hambrough. Henry Littlejohn and Patrick Heron Watson agreed the shot could not be self-inflicted. However, sufficient doubt had been sowed in the minds of the jury by Monson's advocate John Comrie Thompson, who presented Prof Matthew Hay as an expert witness who strongly contradicted the other experts. The jury was not convinced either way, although they agreed that the charges against Monson were rendered plausible by the evidence. Thus, the case was 'not proved', and Monson was set free.

Many people were shocked by the verdict. The eminent crime writer Edgar Wallace wrote, 'that the evidence is 100% for conviction, so the jury was either kind or blind.'

Hanborough's loyal friends were especially shocked by the verdict, and for many years on the anniversary of his death; notices appeared in national newspapers saying, 'Sacred to the memory of Cecil Dudley Hambrough shot in a wood near Ardlamont, August 10, 1893, vengeance is mine. I will repay.'

Bell was involved in several police investigations, usually working alongside Henry Littlejohn, who was also brought into the mix when Conan Doyle created Holmes. (Watson)

Their presence, mainly Bell's, made people interested in the trial's outcome. When they became part of the investigation, people became highly interested in their statements, wondering what the real Sherlock Holmes would say.

A year later, Madame Tussaud's London unveiled a Monson waxwork in the entrance to their Chamber of Horrors, bearing a gun. Monson took exception to this and sued the waxworks for 'libel by innuendo'. Monson was awarded one farthing in damages, the lowest possible amount. This case set a precedent and still forms the basis of defamation and libel law today.

Three years after the infamous Ardlamont mystery, Monson committed further offences and was arrested using the name of Alfred John Wyville. (A popular Filey name) He and the family rented a house on the Isle of Wight, which burned to the ground in mysterious circumstances. This case against him was proven, and Monson was jailed for perjury for eighteen months. Monson then claims five hundred pounds worth of jewellery from the Insurance Companies. A leopard doesn't change its spots!

Soon after, Monson moved to South Africa and changed his name again. Presumably, he died there, although this is impossible to trace without knowing his new name.

Fortunately, Monson and his family did not live in Filey for long, but we presume that he certainly left his mark on the town, and his persona and plot laid the basis for the characters in the Sherlock Holmes books. As for Monson? Was he guilty? Sherlock Holmes certainly thought so.

Filey is truly a magical place. The jewel of the Yorkshire Coast. However, as we have read in this book, many dangers exist from strong tides, dangerous cliffs, or sunburn on the beach. Remember to watch for the incoming tide and be careful always. And don't forget the sunscreen.

*

If you enjoyed reading this book, please consider leaving a review and rating on the site where you purchased it. Please tell your friends about *The History of Filey and its People* and help keep the history of the beautiful town alive. A review helps tremendously.

Thank you

Sources of Information

Thank you for all the excellent resources for help in compiling this book. Many titles are out of print, but several were available from Google's digitised archives. The British Newspaper Archive is a valuable and addictive source for my research. As some photographs are old, their quality is sometimes impaired.

A Historical and Descriptive Guide to Filey. W.S. Cortis. 1858.

Buildings of England, Yorkshire, York and East Riding. Nikolaus Pevsner. Penguin Books. 1972.

Domesday Book and the East Riding. F.W. Brooks. 1966.

Fearon, Michael. *Filey*. 1st Ed. Beverley, East Yorkshire: Hutton, 1990. Print.

Filey and its Church. A.N. Cooper. F.W. Brooks (The Gentleman's Magazine) Accessed online 24/1/2017.

Observations of Filey as a Watering Place. E.W. Pritchard M.D M.R.C.S. George L Beeforth, 3, St Nicholas Street, Scarborough 1858.

Shipwrecks and The Yorkshire Coast. Arthur Godfrey and Peter J Lasey Dalesman Books. 1974.

The Filey Handbook. Rev.Arthur Pettitt MA. Loxley Bros. 1868.

The History & Antiquities of Filey in the County of York. John Cole Printed and Published by J. Cole 1828.

Websites.

"Borthwick Institute for Archives - Borthwick Institute for Archives, The University of York". York. ac. UK. N.p., 2017. (Elinor Clarke)

British Newspaper Archive". Britishnewspaperarchive.co.uk. N.p., 2017. Web. 26 Jan. 2017.

Websites.

https://www.facebook.com/groups/photosoffiley/Accessed 20162017.

"Gristhorpe Man - University of Bradford". Bradford.ac.uk. N.p., 2017. Web. 26 Jan. 2017.

Hull Packet. A Scandalous Woman. Accessed 5/7/2015.

London Evening Standard. 18/2/1857. 'Filey's Iron Church.' Accessed 4/4/2016.

"Matlock And Matlock Bath: Kelly's Directory, 1855". Andrewsgen.com. N.p., 2017. Web. 26 Jan. 2017. (Re Elinor Clarke)

Newcastle Chronicle. 16/3/1866-Filey 'Harbour of Refuge.' Accessed 2/3/2016

The London Gazette. 'Filey Harbour Company.' Accessed 10/5/2016.

Trove. n/a. au/newspaper articles 68721534-Filey Flying. www.myprimitivemethodists.org.uk (Accessed 21/2/2017) www.christianitytoday.com (Accessed 21/2/2017)

Email-

Filey Town Council.

The Jorvik Centre-York. Cockayne, Kevin. Filey. E-mail.

Waterson, Edward-Elinor Clarke-Email-Elinor Clarke.

Theobald, James-Email. Elinor Clarke

www.ingramcontent.com/pod-product-compliance
Lightning Source LLC
Chambersburg PA
CBHW051506030726
47592CB00006B/2124